SPIRITUAL REFLECTIONS

A Journey Through the Scriptures

DR. HENRY G. COVERT

Spiritual Reflections
by Dr. Henry G. Covert

Copyright © 2023
All rights reserved.

All rights reserved. Reproduction or utilization of this work in any form, by any means now known or herein after invented, including but not limited to xerography, photocopying and recording, and in any storage and retrieval system, is forbidden without permission from the copyrighted holder.

Library of Congress Control Number: 2023939526
International Standard Book Number: 978-1-60126-867-9

𝕸𝖆𝖘𝖙𝖍𝖔𝖋 𝕻𝖗𝖊𝖘𝖘
219 Mill Road | Morgantown, PA 19543-9516
www.Masthof.com

To my parents, who always prayed for me and provided the foundations for my spiritual life.
To my wife Kathy, whose encouragement and support have made my ministry possible.
This book is dedicated to everyone who seeks a deeper relationship with the Lord.

CONTENTS

Preface	xiii
Chapter One: Supernatural Love	1
The Greatest Commandments	1
A Life Given	2
Power of the Cross	3
Loving Our Enemies	5
The Good Shepherd	6
Selfless Love	7
What Is Forgiveness?	9
The Test of Spirituality	10
Chapter Two: Faithfulness	13
What Is Faith?	13
God's Faithfulness	14
Faith That Saves	16
Faith in the Present	17
Who Do People Say I Am?	18
Sustaining Grace	20
The Blessings of Faith	21
More Than Conquerors	22
Chapter Three: Trusting in God's Promises	25
Living Stones	25
Bitter Waters	26

Seek the Kingdom First	28
The Sea of Fear	29
Abiding Joy	31
The Skeptic	32
Making Comparisons	33
Chapter Four: Compassion	35
A Compassionate Presence	35
The Call for Mercy	37
Chapter Five: Divine Guidance	39
Teach Us How to Pray	39
Promise of the Holy Spirit	40
The True Manna	41
Cleansing the Temple	42
Chapter Six: The Great Commission	45
The Commission	45
Sent into the World	46
Responding to the Message of Jesus	48
Preparing the Way	49
The Gospel of Reconciliation	50
A Challenging Mission	51
The Body of Christ	53
Chapter Seven: Repentance	55
The Repentant Sinner	55
Call to Repentance	57
Forgetting the Lord	58
Prayers of the Heart	59
Chapter Eight: Facing Trials	63
Reaction to Affliction	63
The Holiness Imperative	65
Lessons from Elijah	66
Choosing Priorities	67
When Depression Comes	69
A Cry for Mercy	70
Trials That Bring Ministry	71
Chapter Nine: Resisting Temptation	75
Enemies of the Cross	75
Remember Lot's Wife	76

Peter's Denial	77
The False Disciple	79
Chapter Ten: Commitment	81
The Vine and Branches	81
A Love Story	82
The Harvest	84
Chapter Eleven: Servanthood	87
Life's Two Paths	87
Making a Decision	88
The Cost of Discipleship	90
Being a Servant	91
Knowing God's Will	92
A Mother's Promise	93
A Lesson on Giving	95
An Eternal Investment	96
Mary Found Favor with God	98
David's Call	100
The Healing Waters	101
A Humble Life	102
Chapter Twelve: Gifts of the Spirit	105
One in Spirit	105
The Content Life	106
What Is Beauty?	107
The Gift of Joy	109
Responses to Truth	110
The Gift of Peace	111
Chapter Thirteen: Transforming Grace	113
Walking in the Spirit	113
Living in the Present	114
Unfailing Love	116
Clouded Vision	117
A Healing and a Warning	118
Chapter Fourteen: Deliverance and Renewal	121
The New Covenant	121
Saving by Losing	122
The New Birth	123
From Death to Life	125

Victory over Death	126
Raising Jairus' Daughter	127
Delivered of Demon Possession	129

Chapter Fifteen: Miracles and Signs — 131
More Than Enough	131
Show Me a Miracle	132
Unseen Realities	133
Seeking Miraculous Signs	135
The Proclamation	136
The Word Became Flesh	137

Chapter Sixteen: Thankfulness — 139
Thankful Hearts	139
Rejoice in the Lord	140
Only One Gave Thanks	141
Sing a New Song	143
Giving Thanks in All Circumstances	144

Chapter Seventeen: Witness for God — 147
A Glowing Witness	147
Christian Lamps	148
A Call to Separation	149
The Model Church	151
Listening and Doing	152

Chapter Eighteen: Disobedience and the End Times — 155
Jonah's Relationships	155
A Sad Funeral	156
The Narrow Door	157
The Reality and Works of Satan	159
Basement Bargaining	161
The Last Days	162

Chapter Nineteen: Hope and Victory — 165
The Race for Victory	165
Promised Blessings	166
Hope Realized	169
Triumph over Temptation	170
Palms of Victory	171
Sorrow for the Dead	172
He Has Risen	174
In a Little While	175

The Heavens Will Shake	176
Eternal Glory	178
Conclusion	181

PREFACE

You are embarking on a spiritual journey that provides insight into the heart and mind of God. Although these biblical accounts and teachings are historical, having been written by inspired writers many years ago, they have contemporary applications. Each text reveals truths that have touched the lives of countless people before us. They reflect the voice of God speaking to humanity, providing the understanding and guidance necessary for righteous living. Through his Word, the Lord offers us forgiveness and a faith relationship that is rooted in Jesus Christ.

It is important that each section be read prayerfully, allowing the Holy Spirit to speak to your personal needs and the uniqueness of your life. One should also give thought to how this devotional material can be communicated to bless the lives of others. I have selected topics that speak to us on different levels, with the objective being personal development and Christian maturity. In a succinct manner, effort was made to explain the cultural settings for the scriptural passages, which will hopefully bring a heightened understanding of the intended lesson.

Let us now receive God's Word, allowing his grace to touch our lives, that we might be transformed and grow in the image of our Savior. Each section should move us to examine our lives and offer to the Lord both our burdens and those areas in our life that need to be changed.

One

SUPERNATURAL LOVE

THE GREATEST COMMANDMENTS

Mark 12:28–31

> One of the teachers of the law came and heard them debating. Noticing that Jesus had given them a good answer, he asked him, "Of all the commandments, which is the most important?" "The most important one," answered Jesus, "is this: 'Hear, O Israel, the Lord our God, the Lord is one. Love the Lord your God with all your heart and with all your soul and with all your mind and with all your strength.' The second is this: 'Love your neighbors as yourself.' There is no commandment greater than these."

A scribe who heard Jesus conversing with the Sadducees came to him wanting to know his understanding of God's greatest commandment. This teacher of the law was impressed with our Savior's discussions, and he gave him a test question. The scribes were the doctors of the law and considered experts on legal matters relating to Judaism. Many of them were members of the Sanhedrin, which was the Jewish Council. As such, the people respected their interpretations of God's Word.

Jesus told his inquisitor that the greatest commandment is the perfect love for God, but he did not stop there. He continued by saying that love for one's neighbor is the second greatest command. Jesus linked the two commands together, indicating that they are inseparable and dependent upon one another. The response given to the scribe was a quote from the Hebrew Bible, for the Lord had given these commandments to Moses. They were to be engraved into the hearts of the people, for within them lie all of God's holy law. It is the rejection of these commandments that leads to sin and human destruction throughout the world.

Our love is the result of God's initiative and mercy. The Lord never gives up on us, and through Jesus Christ he has shown us a sacrificial and infinite love that is beyond our comprehension. It is a love that never ceases to offer hope for a sinful world. Worldly empires built upon force have come and gone, but the kingdom of God cannot be destroyed. When, in faith, we receive God's love, our hearts are changed, and life takes on a new direction. We seek to please the Lord in all that we do, offering our lives in praise and thanksgiving. Although our love for God is imperfect, our intentions can be pure.

Coupled with the greatest commandment is the command to love our neighbors as ourselves. Unlike some individuals who draw a circle of love and exclude certain people, Jesus teaches that neighbors include everyone, even our enemies. Such love, however, is not possible unless God rules our hearts. Shortly before Jesus was crucified he said to his disciples, "A new command I give you, that you love one another, even as I have loved you." The love that took Jesus to the cross was for all people, and it is this unconditional love that we must possess. Jesus gave his love to the cheating tax collectors and harlots. He even loved the nervous Pontius Pilate, who pronounced his death sentence.

After Jesus was arrested in Gethsemane, Peter followed the arresting party to the courtyard of the high priest, where three times he denied knowing his Savior. After Jesus rose from the dead, he came to Peter and asked, "Do you love me?" When Peter acknowledged that he did, Jesus told Peter to love all people by being their shepherd. The commission that was given to Peter is the mission of the Church and all Christians.

A LIFE GIVEN

Mark 15:25–32

> It was the third hour when they crucified him. The written notice of the charge against him read: The King of the Jews. They crucified two robbers with him, one on his right and one on his left. Those who passed by hurled insults at him, shaking their heads and saying, "So! You who are going to destroy the temple and build it in three days, come down from the cross and save yourself!" In the same way, the chief priests and teachers of the law mocked him among themselves. "He saved others," they said, "but he can't save himself! Let this Christ, this King of Israel, come down now from the cross, that we may see and believe." Those crucified with him also heaped insults on him.

The crucifixion of Jesus Christ reveals both the love of God and the sins of humanity. It is the means through which God offers salvation to the world. But rather than believe in the divinity of Jesus and the power of the cross, our Savior's contemporaries saw him as simply another victim of Roman oppression and cruelty. Unfortunately, this belief continues to this day. The crucifixion just doesn't fit into our way of thinking. The world refused to believe then, and people refuse to believe now. What kind of king would willingly be crucified and ask God to forgive his enemies? How can a Roman cross free people from sin?

The Jewish leaders saw Jesus as a misguided teacher who had lost touch with reality. As such, he was causing havoc amongst the populace, which put the positions of the religious elite at risk. They feared that the Roman government might take action to eliminate their authority. But like the religious leaders, the common people also refused to believe that a universal truth was taking place that would forever change humanity. They failed to understand the prophecies that began with the book of Genesis and continued through the prophets. To the intellectuals, salvation through a Roman cross was ludicrous.

But regardless of the disbelief in Jesus, the prophecies were fulfilled. If Jesus' life had been spared, the Scriptures would have been broken with Satan being the victor. Jesus died at Golgotha, the just for the unjust. It was a death that consumed our sins and reconciled us with the Father. When Christ was crucified the world became black and the earth's foundations shook. As the Trinity suffered and death took place within the Godhead, it seemed like the world was coming apart.

The cross is now empty, and so is the tomb where they laid our Lord's body. Jesus both paid our penalty, and he conquered death. He is our living Savior, who holds the keys to life and death. The veil of the temple was rent, and we now have access to the Father through his Son. Although Calvary was an historical event, its truth is eternal. On a Roman cross almost two thousand years ago, hung the life of every sinner. The cross is where sin dies and life begins. It is the sacrificial death of Jesus that restores our humanity by filling us with love, thanksgiving, and praise for God. Have you traveled to the Calvary of forgiveness, and are you living in the forgiveness and power of the Cross?

POWER OF THE CROSS

I Corinthians 1:18–20, 22, 23

> For the message of the cross is foolishness to those who are perishing, but to us who are being saved, it is the power of God. For it is written: "I will destroy the

wisdom of the wise; the intelligence of the intelligent I will frustrate." Where is the wise man? Where is the scholar? Where is the philosopher of this age? Has not God made foolish the wisdom of the world? Jews demand miraculous signs, and Greeks look for wisdom, but we preach Christ crucified, a stumbling block for Jews and foolishness to Gentiles.

There were spiritual problems in the Corinthian church, for some members were following individuals rather than Jesus Christ. Verse twelve reads, "One of you says, I follow Paul; another, I follow Apollos; another, I follow Cephas; still another, I follow Christ." What we see are divisions amongst the people that were leading them away from the teachings of Christ and his atoning sacrifice at Calvary. Paul said, "Is Christ divided? Was Paul crucified for you? Were you baptized into the name of Paul?"

The Christians in Corinth were experiencing both Greek and Hebrew influences, and some of the people had problems accepting the power of the cross. The Jews were a very "matter of fact" type of people, and they demanded evidence and signs. Their interest was always in the practical; therefore, a crucified Messiah was abhorrent to them. How could God's Anointed One die on a Roman cross? The Greeks also had problems with the cross, but it was for other reasons. They were absorbed in speculative philosophy and were seeking the ultimate reality. In their search for the force behind the universe, the cross was simply out of question. What kind of logic is found in a man's execution?

In this letter to the Corinthians, Paul spoke directly to the question of salvation. He said that we cannot compare our wisdom to that of the Lord. He wrote that we are not saved by our wisdom or way of seeing things. In fact, says Paul, God's wisdom is the opposite of ours. The cross of Jesus Christ was foolish during Paul's life, and it remains foolish today to those who are perishing. But God reveals that he will destroy the wisdom of the wise and the intelligence of the intelligent. The Lord says, if you are seeking forgiveness go to Calvary. If you are looking for wisdom, look upon the broken body of my beloved Son. If you desire salvation, it is in the blood of Jesus. The cross is God's wisdom and logic, and the means through which we are saved. We stand before the Lord's bar of justice as guilty sinners, but Jesus has paid the penalty to set us free.

Why is it so difficult for people to accept the sacrificial love of the cross? Jesus said, "A greater love has no one than this, that one lay down his life for his friends." The cross of Jesus reveals the horror of sin, as well as the depth of God's love. Isaiah's prophetic words reinforce the purpose of the crucifixion when he wrote, "He was pierced for our transgressions, he was crushed for our iniquities; the punishment that brought us peace was upon him, and by his wounds we are healed." On the cross Jesus said, "It is finished." What he came to do, he did to the glory of the Father. Pontius Pilate asked Jesus, "What is truth?" If only he knew that he was looking at Truth, and that salvation would come through the death of Jesus.

LOVING OUR ENEMIES

Matthew 5:43–48

> "You have heard that it was said, 'Love your neighbor and hate your enemies.' But I tell you: Love your enemies, and pray for those who persecute you, that you may be sons of your Father in heaven. He causes the sun to rise on the evil and the good, and sends rain on the righteous and the unrighteous. If you love those who love you, what reward will you get? Are not even the tax collectors doing that? And if you greet only your brothers, what are you doing more than others? Do not even pagans do that? Be perfect, therefore, as your heavenly Father is perfect."

Do we really love those whom we perceive to be our enemies? If God were to examine our heart this very moment, what would it reveal? We must admit that our lips do not always mirror our true feelings. It is easy to say that we love our enemies, especially when we know that God requires it, but realities are often quite different. In this passage Jesus challenges our Christianity by asking us to do what is not natural. After all, it is not normal to love people who seek to hurt us. So, how are we to understand this radical teaching? I'm sure we would agree that even Christians tend to place conditions on their love.

Jesus came to earth for the purpose of reaching out to God's enemies. He came as a physician for the sick, seeking to transform those living in sin. During his ministry, our Savior certainly hated humanity's sinful acts, but his love for every sinner was boundless. Jesus died for us while we were still sinners, which is a truth we seem to forget. The heart of Christ was breaking for those who spit upon him and beat him with their fists. He loved those who ripped him open with the whip and forced him to carry his cross along Jerusalem's streets. When his executioners stripped him naked and ruthlessly crucified him, he prayed that the Father would forgive them. Maybe it was this love that the centurion saw that led him to believe that Jesus was no ordinary man. As he was being tortured and killed, Jesus sought God's mercy for his enemies. This is the Jesus who commands that we love our enemies and pray for those who persecute us.

It is the love of Jesus Christ that transforms us, enabling us to draw others to God's throne of forgiveness and grace. If we only love those who love us, we are no different than the secular world. To love people who dislike us reveals the reality of a loving God, who desires that all people be saved. Jesus said that it is by loving our enemies that we become children of God. This is a truth that we seldom hear in Christian circles, including church ministries. Jesus clarified the equality of God's love when he said that the Father causes the sun to rise and the rain to fall on both the righteous and unrighteous. In others words, when it comes to the gifts of life, God shows no partiality between good and evil people.

Jesus tells us to be perfect, as our heavenly Father is perfect. In this context, he is defining perfection as having pure intentions and motives. Amid our imperfections we must pray for this kind of love, that others might know Jesus. The world is full of people who were once enemies of God, but love changed their lives. To be perfect in love is to see everyone as God's child.

THE GOOD SHEPHERD

John 10:7–9, 11, 14, 15

> Jesus said, "I tell you the truth, I am the gate for the sheep. All who ever came before me were thieves and robbers, but the sheep did not listen to them. I am the gate, whoever enters through me will be saved. He will come in and go out and find pasture. I am the good shepherd. The good shepherd lays down his life for the sheep. I am the good shepherd. I know my sheep, and my sheep know me—just as the Father knows me, and I know the Father—and I lay down my life for the sheep."

The Scriptures use the word *shepherd* both literally and figuratively. For example, certain kings and leaders were called shepherds of the people, including King David. In some of the psalms, God is called the Shepherd of Israel, and the prophet Isaiah announced that the Lord would come to his people as a shepherd. The apostle Paul called Jesus the Great Shepherd of the sheep, and Peter refers to him as the Chief Shepherd. Since biblical times the word shepherd has had pastoral significance, that of a compassionate and giving spiritual leader. By assuming this title, Jesus was communicating his caring and giving nature, as well as his saving power.

There are striking comparisons between a shepherd and the life of Jesus Christ. Shepherds live with their sheep, providing for all of their needs. It is a life of total dedication in which the sheep come first. This is the life that Jesus has given us. Our Savior left his throne of glory that we might come into his fold, where he can give us his divine love and care. As Jesus called the first disciples into his fold, he also gathers us through his offer of forgiveness. He seeks out the lost and rejoices when they are found and brought into his care. The parable of the Prodigal Son exemplifies the joy of those who are found and return to the Father's house. Our Lord is on an endless search, always calling and gathering his lost sheep.

As the Great Shepherd, Jesus not only provides for his sheep, but he also leads us out of sin and into a righteous life of service. It is a life that is quickened by the Holy Spirit and fed with God's Word. Shepherds of the field are known to protect their sheep from predators, even to the point of laying down their life if necessary. This reveals another spiritual truth, for in Jesus Christ we have a Shepherd who was willing to lay down his life that we might be saved from the enemy. The apostle Paul said that Jesus is truly the Great Shepherd of the sheep, who has given everything within him to protect and save us from a world that seeks our spiritual demise.

Psalm twenty-three, which has universally been attributed to King David, provides a powerful imagery of God as the Shepherd of the people. This writing reveals the Lord as the fount of all blessings. Although it does not suggest an easy life for the sheep, it does assure us of God's vigilance and eternal care. David knew that whatever trial he faced, the Lord was there to give him strength and victory. Whether in life or death, he was confident that God would never leave him. He realized that the Lord was his rock and refuge, and he surrendered his life to his care.

A unique characteristic of sheep is their total dependence upon the shepherd. They place their trust in the one who has devoted their life to them. The sheep do not respond to strangers, knowing the potential dangers that exist. The shepherd lives with them and has always met their needs, and the sheep feel safe in the shepherd's presence. Have we truly placed our lives in the care of our Great Shepherd, trusting him in all circumstances?

SELFLESS LOVE

John 12:1–8

> Six days before the Passover, Jesus arrived in Bethany, where Lazarus lived, who Jesus had raised from the dead. Here a dinner was given in Jesus' honor. Martha served, while Lazarus was among those reclining at the table with him. Then Mary took about a pint of pure nard, an expensive perfume; she poured it on Jesus' feet and wiped his feet with her hair. And the house was filled with the

fragrance of the perfume. But one of the disciples, Judas Iscariot, who was later to betray him, objected, "Why wasn't this perfume sold and the money given to the poor? It was worth a year's wages." He did not say this because he cared about the poor but because he was a thief; as keeper of the money bag, he used to help himself to what was put in it. "Leave her alone," Jesus replied. "It was meant that she should save this perfume for the day of my burial. You will always have the poor among you, but you will not always have me."

According to the accounts given by Matthew and Mark, the supper given in Jesus' honor was at the house of Simon the leper, whom Jesus had healed. Martha, who was the sister of Lazarus, helped serve the meal. This was probably a two-family effort to give thanks to Jesus for both his healing of Simon and raising of Lazarus from the dead. We are told that this occasion took place six days before the Passover, which means just six days before Jesus' crucifixion.

As we examine this passage, we first note Mary's love for Jesus and the sacrificial gift that she gave him. This was met with Judas' criticism, followed by our Lord's justification for what she did. While others were content to simply be in Jesus' presence, Mary felt the need to reach out to Jesus, whose love and forgiveness had changed her life. Not only did she humble herself by anointing his feet and wiping them with her hair, but also she used an expensive perfume that, according to Judas, was worth a year's wages. But for Mary, the costlier the better, for she wanted her Lord to have the best that she could give him. She gave Jesus her worldly treasure, and then she laid her soul at his feet. Her love offering was experienced by everyone in the room, for the perfume filled the air.

Judas told Jesus that the perfume should have been sold, and the money given to the poor. His concern, however, was not for the poor, but rather for himself. He was the keeper of the money and often helped himself to what was collected for the ministry. He saw no glory in Mary's act of love and the attention that she gave to Jesus. Unfortunately, many people today would respond in the same manner. After all, a year's wages is a significant amount of money to waste. But Jesus wanted everyone to know that no gift is wasted on him, and that he must be first in our lives.

This scripture passage gives us a beautiful picture of what it means to sacrificially give to the Lord. It is an example of a servant in love with her Savior, as well as an expression of love that makes us look at ourselves. Do we give to God out of our poverty or surplus? Does our love for Jesus move us to become his servants? Is there the desire to bow before him in humility and praise? When Mary met Jesus, she knew that nothing was more important than her relationship with him. I wonder how many professing Christians feel this way, realizing that apart from the grace that flows through Jesus Christ we would have nothing. We talk about love and giving, but what does our life really reflect? What are we willing to give to the one who gave his life for us?

WHAT IS FORGIVENESS?

Matthew 18:21, 22

> Then Peter came to Jesus and asked, "Lord, how many times shall I forgive my brother when he sins against me? Up to seven times?" Jesus answered, "I tell you, not seven times, but seventy-seven times."

The sacrificial life and death of Jesus is about forgiveness; God forgiving us and we forgiving one another. But what does it mean to forgive another person? Is it possible to forget what another person has done to us? Forgiveness is an attitude of the heart that begins with desire and continues with prayer. Although we may not necessarily forget a hurtful situation, we are called to pray for a pure heart that is void of anger and malice.

The ancient Jewish rabbis taught that a person was not to forgive someone beyond three times, and Peter more than doubled that, believing that he was being generous. Little did he know the response Jesus would give him. Our Savior wanted Peter to know that forgiveness has no limit. As Christians, we must always be ready to forgive those who offend us. Like many people today, Peter failed to understand the depth of forgiveness, and we can be certain that Jesus' response shook the foundations of his belief system.

The only recorded words written by Jesus were scratched in the ground, and they concerned the forgiveness of a woman caught in adultery, which was an act punishable by death at that time. But, our Lord's words and actions forced her male accusers to examine their own lives, and after doing so they were unwilling to pursue their accusations. It is interesting how we sometimes fail to see our sins and the need for continuing grace. It is God's nature to forgive everyone who comes to him with a repentant heart. This is our Savior's message, and the one proclaimed by the apostles. Paul told the Ephesians that they must love and forgive one another, just as in Christ, God forgave their sins. How can we expect God to forgive us, if we refuse to forgive others? In the Lord's Prayer we seek God's forgiveness while acknowledging our forgiveness of other people. Jesus takes this a step farther, telling us that unless we forgive one another, we will not be forgiven by God. He also teaches that we must pray for our enemies, which is the real test of discipleship. Let us never forget, that in the midst of his agonizing death, Jesus prayed for his enemies.

The Scriptures report that a paralytic came to Jesus to be healed. However, before the Lord healed the stricken man, he told him that his sins were forgiven. What a strange response to a man who simply asked to be cured. But Jesus wanted the man to know that forgiveness takes precedence over everything, for it speaks to the eternal soul. Forgiveness mends lives and brings emotional and spiritual healing, all of which address our present relationships and our reconciliation with God.

Do you have the desire to forgive individuals who sin against you, including those believed to be your enemy? If so, do you continuously pray for the heart of Christ? Forgiveness is only possible when we possess the love and sacrificial life of our Savior.

THE TEST OF SPIRITUALITY

Romans 8:1–8

> Therefore, there is now no condemnation for those who are in Christ Jesus, because through Christ Jesus the law of the Spirit of life set me free from the law of sin and death. For what the law was powerless to do, in that it was weakened by the sinful nature, God did by sending his own Son in the likeness of sinful man to be a sin offering. And so he condemned sin in the sinful man, in order that the righteous requirements of the law might be fully met in us, who do not live in the sinful nature but according to the Spirit. Those who live according to the sinful nature have their minds set on what that nature desires; but those who live in accordance with the Spirit have their minds set on what the Spirit desires. The mind of the sinful man is death, but the mind controlled by the Spirit is life and peace, because the sinful mind is hostile to God. It does not submit to God's law, nor can it do so. Those controlled by the sinful nature cannot please God.

Paul's epistle to the Romans holds deep theological thoughts and truths, some of which are difficult to comprehend. Although this passage is in that category, it is one that should be examined. In this letter to the Christians in Rome, Paul is making a comparison between the life of the Spirit and one that is controlled by the sinful nature. He first states that those in Christ are not condemned, meaning that they are not guilty before God. While they are certainly not sinless, their life is ruled by the Holy Spirit. Rather than being controlled by sin, as they previously were, their faith in Christ has set them free.

Paul also wrote that because of the sinful nature, the law lacks power. In terms of obedience and righteous living, the law can only do so much. What is needed is a changed heart, which is only possible through Jesus Christ. It is the heart of Christ in us that enables us to obey God in the spirit of love. In this life perfection is not possible, but the Lord honors the pure heart that continuously strives for righteousness. Paul wrote, "For what the law was powerless to do, in that it was weakened by the sinful nature, God did by sending his own Son in the likeness of sinful man to be a sin offering." We are forgiven through the sacrifice of Jesus, and we have power over intentional sin through the indwelling presence of the Holy Spirit. Our faith in Jesus as Lord and Savior brings these realities into our lives.

This brief lesson tells us that real spirituality is not simply obedience out of a sense of obligation or fear. Instead, it is a changed heart that is realized through faith and a surrendered life. Paul told the believers in Rome that those who walk in the Spirit have their minds set on what the Spirit desires. They pray for the love and humility of Jesus, and they look to the interests of others. The test of spirituality relates to the changes that have taken place in our lives. Do we seek the things of God, or do we still covet that which the world offers? Only when we allow the Holy Spirit full reign over our lives do we share in the nature of Christ.

We live in a world in which everything is fine-tuned, and that is the way we like it. But, what about our hearts? King David asked the Lord to search out his heart for any area of unrighteousness. How many people do this? We must frequently examine our thoughts and actions, for they reveal the condition of our hearts. Those who do not command their thoughts will soon lose control of their actions.

Two

FAITHFULNESS

WHAT IS FAITH?

I John 5:4

> For everyone born of God has overcome the world. This is the victory that has overcome the world, even our faith. Who is it that overcomes the world? Only he who believes that Jesus Christ is the Son of God.

The Scriptures teach that we are saved by God's grace and our personal faith in Jesus Christ. Although the word *faith* is found in our everyday vocabulary, how should we understand it in terms of our relationship with God and others? Saint Augustine provides the following insights:

Faith is the foot of the soul—it runs to Christ.
Faith is the hand of the soul—it receives Christ.
Faith is the arm of the soul—it embraces Christ.
Faith is the eye of the soul—it looks upon Christ.
Faith is the mouth of the soul—it feeds upon Christ.

We have all heard the secular expressions relating to faith, and in the spiritual realm there are many educational tools that focus upon this subject. But the faith that we are concerned about relates to our salvation, specifically our trust in God for things that we have not yet received. Saint Augustine said that "faith is found in what we do not yet see, and the reward of faith is to ultimately see what we have believed." Emerson wrote, "All that I have seen teaches me to trust the Creator for all that I have not seen." The apostle Paul wrote that "faith is being sure of what we hope for and certain of what we do not see." He said that the ancients were commended for this. So, faith is absolute trust within the context of the unseen and what we have not yet received.

Paul wrote that those who are righteous before God live by faith, rather than the human reasoning that many people follow. But, how do we receive this faith? Like all gifts, the faith that brings salvation and spiritual nurturing, is given to us through desire, persistent prayer, and daily application. The seeds of faith take root when we reach out and receive Jesus as our Lord and Savior, and our faith grows as we apply it in our daily lives. Like our physical bodies that become weak due to a lack of exercise, one's faith experiences the same thing. Just as there are sagging bodies, there is also sagging faith.

We have no idea what lies ahead of us, but the Lord sees the entire road map and is able to guide us through the detours and the twists and turns. Jesus emphasizes that we must have the innocent faith of a child. Even during the worst of times, children somehow believe that their parents will get them through adversity. Many adults still have this type of relationship with their parents. The Lord wants us to come to him as the little children that we are, seeking his strength, wisdom, and guidance.

We must pray for the desire and ability to trust God, thereby enabling us to set aside pride and self-will. This includes asking the Lord for the strength to exercise our faith, so that it may continue to grow. Like the mustard seed, which grows into a large tree-like shrub, we need to pursue a growing faith that is deeply rooted in God. If you recall, Jesus taught Thomas a lesson on faith. Thomas said to the other disciples, "Unless I see the nail marks in his hands and put my finger where the nails were, and put my hand into his side, I will not believe that Jesus rose from the dead." Jesus later appeared to Thomas and said, "Put your finger here; see my hands. Reach out your hand and put it into my side. Stop doubting and believe." Then Jesus said to him, "Because you have seen me, you have believed; blessed are those who have not seen and yet have believed."

GOD'S FAITHFULNESS

Psalm 73:1–5, 13, 14, 16, 17, 21–25

> Surely God is good to Israel, to those who are pure in heart. But as for me, my feet had almost slipped; I had nearly lost my foothold. For I envied the arrogant, when I saw the prosperity of the wicked. They have no struggles; their bodies

are healthy and strong. They are free from the burdens common to man; they are not plagued by human ills. Surely, in vain have I kept my heart pure; in vain have I washed my hands in innocence. All day long I have been plagued; I have been punished every morning. When I tried to understand all this, it was oppressive to me, till I entered the sanctuary of God; then I understood their final destiny. When my heart was grieved and my spirit embittered I was senseless and ignorant; I was a brute beast before you. Whom have I in heaven but you? And being with you, I desire nothing on earth.

This psalm was written by Asaph, who was a Levite and musician appointed by King David to preside over the sacred choral services in the temple. The words and tone of this writing speak to us, for they address questions of fairness and justice in this life. Have you ever compared yourself to those who seem to have it all? Why is it that so many people who have no regard for the Lord do well in life? I am certain that many of God's faithful servants have experienced this frustration. Try as they may, there is always another mountain to climb.

Asaph saw the prosperity of the wicked, that they were free of the burdens and struggles that the common person had to endure. He believed that they were arrogant and wore their pride like a necklace. What was really troubling was how others were attracted to such people. Who could understand this injustice, and where does God enter into the picture? Is there a contradiction between the Lord's promises and the realities of life? The psalmist initially believed this to be true, and he was about to give up. He said, "When I tried to understand all this, it was oppressive to me." With limited understanding and vision we sometimes develop these feelings. While we have physical eyesight, our spiritual vision is often blurred. We still love God, but we question the injustices in this world. This causes us to cry out to the Lord for answers. Asaph had reached this point, saying, "In vain have I washed my hands in innocence." It was only after Asaph entered God's sanctuary that he saw a different picture of life and death.

While in the Lord's temple, Asaph began to understand the plight of those who reject the Lord, while flaunting their wealth and power. He was reminded of the brevity of this life, and that the situation of the wicked was temporary. He was provided insight into the judgment and destiny of the wicked, as well as the eternal bliss of the righteous. Then he said to God, "I was senseless and ignorant; I was a brute beast before you. Whom have I in heaven but you? And being with you, I desire nothing on earth." It was in the Lord's sanctuary that Asaph's anger and pain was overcome with peace and joy. The apostle Paul tells us that the glory that lies ahead will completely erase the suffering of this present age. We are not to envy the unrighteous or covet what other people possess, for this life is but a flash of light in the context of eternity. Our rewards will be fulfilled when the race is finished, and they will last forever. In the meantime, God's grace will provide peace and strength, along with a life of purpose and fulfillment.

FAITH THAT SAVES

Mark 11:20–26

> In the morning, as they went along, they saw a fig tree withered from the roots. Peter remembered and said to Jesus, "Rabbi, look! The fig tree you cursed has withered!" "Have faith in God," Jesus answered. "I tell you the truth, if anyone says to this mountain, 'Go, throw yourself into the sea,' and does not doubt in his heart but believes that what he says will happen, it will be done for him. Therefore I tell you, whatever you ask for in prayer, believe that you have received it, and it will be yours. And when you stand praying, if you hold anything against anyone, forgive him, so that your Father in heaven may forgive you your sins."

Did you ever try to move a mountain through faith and prayer? Don't be surprised when nothing happens, and begin questioning your faith. In this lesson Jesus is using hyperbole, an exaggerated figure of speech intended to get a person's attention. This is not to suggest, however, that it lacks truth. So, what kind of mountain is Jesus speaking about? He is alluding to the mountains of life, meaning those obstacles and trials that stand in our way as we seek after righteousness and God's will. Life is full of mountains, but through persistent faith and prayer we can be victorious.

Life's mountains come in many forms, such as fear, depression, the lack of self-worth, and hopelessness, to mention a few. They may also surface through deep personal loss, such as the death of a loved one. But Jesus tells us to have faith, for in him we can move the mountains that would hinder us from living happy and fulfilled lives. Regardless of what the impasse may be, in Christ we have the resources to work through life's challenges. Jesus told his disciples to follow him in faith, which requires that we allow him to lead us through life's rough terrain. We will never know what is around the corner or over the next hill, but the Lord looks down upon our lives and knows the obstacles and dangers along the way. As you know, the roadways of life have a way of completely changing the direction of our lives.

Verse twenty-five of our text is crucial to our teaching, for it addresses the importance of relationships when making our requests known to God.

It reads, "When you stand praying, if you hold anything against anyone, forgive him, so that your Father in heaven may forgive you your sins." Before offering up our petitions with the expectation of God's response, we must examine our relationships, being certain that we are not harboring anything against another person. The Lord does not respond to an unforgiving person, nor can the Holy Spirit move through the life of someone who refuses to forgive others. People seldom give thought to their relationships and how they impact upon their prayer life and spiritual formation.

Faith in Jesus Christ, combined with a forgiving heart, begins the journey that carries us to the Father's house. The apostle Paul tells us that salvation is a matter of faith from beginning to end. In other words, we are to live out our faith each day, while awaiting our Savior's return. Faith is the victory that overcomes the world. We are called to trust in our Creator's wisdom, and to stand firm on our Savior's teachings.

FAITH IN THE PRESENT

John 11:38–44

> Jesus, once more deeply moved, came to Lazarus' tomb. It was a cave with a stone laid across the entrance. "Take away the stone," he said. "But, Lord," said Martha, the sister of the dead man, "by this time there is a bad odor, for he has been there for four days." Then Jesus said, "Did I not tell you that if you believed, you would see the glory of God?" So they took away the stone. Then Jesus looked up and said, "Father, I thank you that you have heard me. I knew that you always hear me, but I did this for the benefit of the people standing here, that they may believe that you sent me." When he had said this, Jesus called in a loud voice, "Lazarus, come out!" The dead man came out, his hands and feet wrapped with strips of linen, and a cloth around his face. Jesus said to them, "Take off the grave clothes and let him go."

After Lazarus died, his sister Martha revealed her faith in his future resurrection at the end of the age. But Jesus had other plans, which would test her faith in the present. What Martha and the others were about to witness would change their lives, for they would see the Lord's glory and power in the present. When Jesus raised Lazarus from the dead, they suddenly realized that faith in God's power is not simply to be understood in the past or future, but rather in our daily lives.

What a story to revive our faith! This happy home in Bethany was overshadowed with deep sorrow over Lazarus' death. His sisters, Martha and Mary, had called Jesus when Lazarus was ill. However, when Jesus heard of his friend's illness, he stayed where he was for two more days. Then Jesus received the message that he need not come because Lazarus had died. But Jesus went to Bethany that he might reveal God's resurrection power and bring comfort to the family. He knew that the resurrection of Lazarus' deteriorating body would erase any doubt of his divinity.

In the midst of Martha's grief, Jesus asked her if she believed in him, and this is the same question that our Savior asks us. When sorrow overcomes us, do we trust God's grace? Do we have faith that when physical death occurs, there is eternal life through Jesus Christ? Even when miracles do not take place, are we leaning upon the promise of God's presence? Martha said to Jesus, "Lord, if you had been here, my brother would not have died." But Jesus was always there, just as he is always with us. There is no need to think of the past or look into the future, for we are promised God's grace in the present. Martha's struggle did not concern the future, for she believed that in the Lord's timing there would be a resurrection of the dead. Her problem was having faith in the present. It is during times of pain that we most often waver in our faith, but Jesus promises never to leave or forsake us. We need to remember that life's trials are spiritual battles that must be confronted with the Word, faith, and prayer. As Paul tells us, to be victorious we need the full armor of God.

We can expect challenging times, but in Jesus Christ we have a refuge. Who else knows human suffering more than our Savior, and who but Jesus has the compassion and power to sustain us? Paul's life was full of disappointments, tragedy, and suffering, but his faith enabled him to see God's presence in all that he endured. We live in the present, and it is in that present that we need faith and power. Suffering is a part of our world, which even Jesus did not escape. But our Lord chooses to be there during our darkest hours, offering his comfort and strength in the present.

WHO DO PEOPLE SAY I AM?

Mark 8:27–29

> Jesus and his disciples went on to the villages around Caesarea Philippi. On the way he asked them, "Who do people say I am?" They replied, "Some say John the Baptist; others say Elijah; and still others, one of the prophets." "But what about you?" he asked. "Who do you say I am?" Peter answered, "You are the Christ."

Jesus presented his apostles with a profound and far-reaching question that focused upon his nature and mission. "Who do people say that I am?" It was an inquiry that was meant to test the faith and understanding of the people.

Jesus wanted to know what the people were saying about him, especially those who had heard his teachings and possibly witnessed some of his miracles. According to the apostles, some people believed that John the Baptist, Elijah, or one of the prophets had come back to life. If this were the case, it meant that God was about to do something miraculous for the people.

Who was this Jesus of Nazareth, who was always accused of violating Jewish laws and stirring up the people? Who was this charismatic, yet unassuming man who seemed to speak with the authority of God? Who was this itinerant preacher who could heal the sick, control the forces of nature, and even raise the dead? Our Savior's question initially focused upon the crowds that were following him. He wanted to know how far they were from the kingdom of God. But then, Jesus turned to his apostles and made the question personal. "Who do you say that I am?" While the other disciples hesitated, probably in a state of wonder or shock, Peter blurted out a response. "You are the Christ," he said, which was an acknowledgment that Jesus was the Messiah sent by God.

The apostles lived with Jesus for approximately three years, listening to his every word. They observed his prayer life and studied his responses to people and life situations. They were conquered by his love, and they rested in his words of forgiveness and eternal life. Jesus was like no one they had ever met. Why else would they leave everything behind to follow him, even risking their lives to be his companion and messengers of his gospel? These men saw in Jesus what they thought was the reflection of God.

The question Jesus asked his disciples is as pertinent today as it was almost two thousand years ago. Who is Jesus for us today? How have his teachings affected our lives? Over the centuries countless people have claimed that Jesus Christ changed their lives. But we have not seen him in the flesh, nor were we witnesses to biblical events. Isn't it true, however, that people continue to be changed by the power of Christ?

Pontius Pilate asked the people, "What shall I do with this Jesus, who is called Christ?" The response given to Pilate was immediate, and Jesus was sentenced to death. But Pilate did not want Jesus put to death, nor did his wife, who had a troubling dream about him. Even the Roman centurion in charge of the execution realized that Jesus was no ordinary man. In fact, when experiencing the earthquake and the events surrounding his death, the centurion acknowledged Jesus as the Son of God.

Although many people have acknowledged the divinity of Jesus, few people have taken up the cross to walk the path of Christ. As we contemplate the question Jesus asked his disciples, we must examine our lives. Do we really believe that Jesus is the Savior of the world? If so, does our life reflect this truth?

SUSTAINING GRACE

II Corinthians 12:2, 4, 5, 7–10

> I know a man in Christ who fourteen years ago was caught up to the third heaven—to Paradise. He heard inexpressible things, that a man is not permitted to tell. I will boast about a man like that, but I will not boast about myself, except about my weaknesses. To keep me from becoming conceited because of these surpassingly great revelations, there was given me a thorn in my flesh, a messenger of Satan, to torment me. Three times I pleaded with the Lord to take it away from me. But he said to me, "My grace is sufficient for you, for my power is made perfect in weakness." Therefore I will boast all the more gladly about my weaknesses, so that Christ's power may rest on me. That is why, for Christ's sake, I delight in weaknesses, in insults, in hardships, in persecutions, in difficulties. For when I am weak, then I am strong.

The apostle Paul is relating a personal experience that he had, telling us that he was caught up to the third heaven, which he calls Paradise. In Paul's day, the third heaven was believed to be beyond the galaxies and the place where God was found in all his glory. Paul could not say whether he made this journey in his spirit, or whether it was both body and spirit. He did know, however, that he was in the realm of the Almighty, and that he was forbidden to report what he saw.

This revelation was given to Paul for a reason, which was probably to strengthen his faith in light of the intense persecution that he would endure for Christ and the gospel. By using the third person in reporting this experience, Paul wanted all attention taken away from him, that God might be glorified. A look at Paul's life and ministry reveals that his journey to Paradise did strengthen his faith, giving him the power to spread the gospel and complete his mission before being martyred in Rome.

But what was this thorn in the flesh that caused Paul such pain? We can only speculate, but many scholars believe that it was an injury Paul sustained. It may have resulted when he was beaten with rods or stoned, which he mentions in this second letter to the Corinthians. Paul states that he prayed on three occasions, asking the Lord for relief. However, instead of removing the pain, God told Paul that he would receive the grace necessary to endure this trial. The Lord assured him that divine power is made perfect in human weaknesses. All Paul needed was faith, and God would provide the necessary grace. It was this chronic pain that kept Paul close to God, enabling him to experience the fullness of God's power. In the Garden of Gethsemane, Jesus also prayed that the cup of suffering would pass him by. When the

Father's answer was clear, Jesus received the grace to endure his excruciating death.

Regardless of what the trial may be, we also can experience the fullness of God's power, if we empty ourselves and allow the Spirit to take control. We must become valleys that soak up divine grace, a reality that comes through faith and prayer. May we never forget that in the midst of our weaknesses and pain, there is a merciful God. In Jesus Christ we have a Savior who can identify with all human suffering, and this arouses his compassion and power. We can be certain that Paul did not look for ways to suffer, but he knew that God's grace is found in every hardship and trial. He understood life's difficulties as an avenue for personal growth, as well as an opportunity to be a witness for his faith.

Life contains many thorns, some of which are very painful. This apparently was the situation with Paul, as evidenced in his prayers for relief. But Paul did not lash out at God, nor did he ever complain or waver in his faith. Rather than question the Lord, he drew closer to him, knowing where his strength and victory was found. For Paul, the power of Christ in his life was more important than freedom from pain, and it was this that he boasted about. Christians are not removed from suffering, but our Savior's disciples know that every trial makes room for God's mercy and power. It is this indwelling power that ignites our faith and brings us closer to the Lord.

THE BLESSINGS OF FAITH

Genesis 12:1–4

> The Lord had said to Abram, "Leave your country, your people and your father's household, and go to the land I will show you. I will make you into a great nation, and I will bless you; I will make your name great, and you will be a blessing. I will bless those who bless you, and whoever curses you I will curse; and all the peoples on earth will be blessed through you." So Abram left, as the Lord had told him; and Lot went with him. Abram was seventy-five years old when he set out for Haran.

Can you imagine being seventy-five years old and asked to leave your country and your people for an unknown future? God called Abram to leave a secure life and travel to a foreign country, where somehow he would be blessed. The Lord told him that he would be the father of a great nation. Although this seems like an incentive to pack up and leave home, Abram had no idea how God's plans would impact upon his life. For example, how much sacrifice would be required on Abram's part, and would there be trials and suffering?

God also told Abram that he would be a blessing to others. What did this mean, and how would it come to fruition? How could the life of one man have a positive influence on generations that did not even exist? And what is even more puzzling is that the Lord called him at the age of seventy-five. But if you recall, he did live to the ripe old age of one hundred and seventy-five years. The fact that he would live this long was also unknown when God asked him to leave his country. There was absolutely no way to understand all of this, for who can know the mind of the Almighty. Although Abram trusted in divine providence and grace, it did not eliminate questions and anxiety. We may trust the Lord, but we still experience the emotions that are attached to life's changes.

Do we ever give thought to how God blesses our faith? Sometimes when we look back upon our lives we realize how we were blessed, but seeing the blessings of faith in the present are more difficult. To understand how we can be a future blessing to others is also difficult to grasp. But this is exactly what God was telling Abram. Can we ever know how our lives will impact upon others? While this may be impossible, we can be assured that our obedience to God will always touch humanity. Whenever we walk in faith, the fruits of our life result in ministry to other people.

Abram was called by the Lord to be a vessel of mercy, and in the process he was also blessed. He is not only our example of faith, but Jesus came to us through his lineage. This truth is revealed in Matthew's genealogy of Jesus Christ. Just think, through Abram's faith and obedience came God's plan for humanity. The Scriptures will forever declare the blessings given to us through this one man, who stepped out on a journey of faith.

Like the Lord called Abram, he beckons us to leave the past behind, to travel to places unknown, and to be the salt of the earth. This may involve moving beyond our circle of family and friends, that we might be blessed and be a blessing to others.

MORE THAN CONQUERORS

Romans 8:31–35, 37–39

> If God is for us, who can be against us? He who did not spare his own Son, but gave him up for us all—how will he not also, along with him, graciously give us all things? Who will bring any charge against those who God has chosen? It is God who justifies. Who is he that condemns? Christ Jesus, who died—more than that, who was raised to life—is at the right hand of God and is also

interceding for us. Who shall separate us from the love of Christ? Shall trouble or hardship or persecution or famine or nakedness or danger or sword? No, in all these things we are more than conquerors through him who loved us. For I am convinced that neither death nor life, neither angels nor demons, neither the present nor the future, nor any powers, neither height nor depth, nor anything else in all creation will be able to separate us from the love of God that is found in Christ Jesus our Lord.

The apostle Paul has provided us with some powerful claims relating to Jesus, but do we believe them? Are we confident that God not only brings us through life's trials, but that in the process we become more than conquerors? Paul was convinced that regardless of what we are going through, God's grace will sustain us and bring victory. He was also assured that we can become more than conquerors, meaning that the faithful will be molded into the image of Christ. Those who face life's difficulties with the Lord, not only get through the difficult times, but they become stronger and more compassionate people. This, of course, speaks to their spiritual life and service to God. Whatever the challenge or depth of pain, Paul believed that the Lord will give his grace and power to those who love him.

We have all experienced those times when we feel overwhelmed with stressful situations. Some individuals and families have one trial after another. Before they recover from one tragedy, another one confronts them. During my years in the ministry, I have been involved in many family struggles. Whether they were relational, financial, medical, or deep personal loss, the pain that people experience can be devastating. During such times it is difficult to grasp what Paul is saying in this passage of scripture. In fact, when we are in the middle of trying times we often feel alone, not even having the desire to pray. But for people who do pray and place their trust in God, there is a well of strength and comfort that is available to them.

While reflecting upon Paul's words, I was reminded of a tragedy that took place in one of my parishes. Late one evening a tornado struck our small community, resulting in the death of two young girls in our congregation. Although there were many individuals who were injured, these two deaths were obviously the most painful. One cannot verbalize the suffering of the families, but what was astonishing was the faith revealed by the parents of one of the girls. In fact, as the months went by, they became deeply involved in the ministry, being a witness of God's healing grace and power. Rather than being angry at God and withdrawing from the church, they shared how the Lord was working in their lives. Although they would continue to experience the pain of their loss, they became more than conquerors.

Three

TRUSTING IN GOD'S PROMISES

LIVING STONES

I Peter 2:4, 5

> As you come to him, the living Stone—rejected by men but chosen by God and precious to him—you also, like living stones, are being built into a spiritual house to be a holy priesthood, offering spiritual sacrifices acceptable to God through Jesus Christ.

In this epistle to scattered Christians, Peter refers to Jesus as a Living Stone sent by God, who was rejected by the people. Throughout the Hebrew Bible the word *stone* or *rock* is used figuratively to describe one of the Lord's characteristics. King David often referred to God as his Rock, in whom he derived his strength and took refuge. In the New Testament, Jesus is called the Cornerstone. The Jews were familiar with the purpose of cornerstones, for they tied construction walls together, providing strength to an entire structure. This was particularly true with the construction of the temple in Jerusalem.

Peter tells us that our lives must be built upon the strength of a cornerstone, who is Jesus Christ. The prophet Isaiah wrote, "So this is what the sovereign Lord says: See, I lay a stone in Zion, a tested stone, a precious cornerstone for a sure foundation; the one who trusts will never be dismayed." It is by trusting in God's Cornerstone that we become an immovable part of God's kingdom. Peter knew the spiritual application of a stone, for Jesus changed his name from Simon to Peter. The name Peter in Greek means *rock*, and it was given to him because of his strong faith. Even though Peter had his weaknesses, Jesus knew that his character was like granite, and when chiseled and molded, he would be a strong witness and leader of the Church.

What are the characteristics of a living stone? Like natural stones, they are solid, with a strong interior. While society looks at the exterior, God probes the inner person, searching out the heart. Many individuals appear to be solid Christians, for they have the exterior that seems to correspond to a changed life. But the outer life of many people is an illusion, for within lies pride and self-centeredness. Living stones possess a strength that is grounded in the teachings of Jesus. They endure the storms, knowing where their hope and victory is found. In spite of the trials, they allow themselves to be continuously molded by God, trusting in his wisdom and grace. They also possess a beauty that attracts others through their radiating glow.

Peter wasn't always a living stone, but he had the potential to become one. He showed a warm attachment to Jesus, opening himself up to our Savior's teachings and example. Peter gave his all to the Lord, and he received the fullness of God's grace. This is the life that Jesus offers everyone who will believe and follow him. Rather than spiritual complacency and simply going through the motions, we are called to be living stones for Jesus Christ. Through prayer and a surrendered life, we can become strong in our faith and commitment.

BITTER WATERS

Exodus 15:22–26

> Then Moses led Israel from the Red Sea, and they went into the Desert of Shur. For three days they traveled in the desert without finding water. When they came to Marah, they could not drink its water because it was bitter. (That is why the place is called Marah.) So the people grumbled against Moses, saying, "What are we to drink?" Then Moses cried out to the Lord, and the Lord showed him a piece of wood. He threw it into the water, and the water became sweet. There the Lord made a decree and a law for them, and there he tested them. He said, "If you listen carefully to the voice of the Lord your God and do what is right in his eyes, if you pay attention to his commands and keep all his decrees, I will not bring on you any of the diseases I brought on the Egyptians, for I am the Lord who heals you."

Have you ever realized how easy it is to have faith when everything is going well, or when you are delivered from some trial? In the fifteenth chapter of Exodus you will discover what I am talking about, for in these verses is the Song of Moses. It was a great triumphant song of the people, in which they celebrated victory over Egyptian bondage. But it wasn't long before the people began grumbling and showing a lack of faith in both Moses and the Lord. Isn't it peculiar that in one instance there were songs of praise and thanksgiving, and shortly thereafter there was complaining, disbelief, and anger. Humanity is strange indeed, for there is a fine line between our songs of praise and our faithless dissatisfaction.

After the joyful song of victory, there was a bitter experience at Marah that tested the faith of the people. In the harsh desert environment there was the need for water, but when the Israelites came to Marah they found that the stream was polluted. At this point the people began to grumble, believing that Moses had brought them into the wilderness to die. When considering that there were 600,000 men, not including women and children, one can imagine the situation that confronted Moses. He had to do something quickly, and the only solution was to desperately cry out to the Lord for help. While over one million people angrily complained, Moses prayed for a miracle. The Lord answered his prayer, but it was an unusual response. God led Moses to a piece of wood, telling him to throw it into the water to purify it. But why didn't God simply use his power to make the water clean?

It seems that God wanted to reaffirm the leadership of Moses in front of the people. He wanted them to once again trust Moses for the long journey that was ahead of them. When Moses threw the wood into the water, it was a confirmation that God was in communion with him. Who could possibly lead over a million people through a long desert journey if they don't trust you as their leader? The Lord also wanted Moses to step out in faith, for he was becoming weary and began to doubt God's presence and his own leadership.

From the construction of this passage, the piece of wood used by Moses was apparently close by. This suggests a spiritual truth, for God's remedies are always close at hand. All that is needed are prayers of faith that seek God's mercy and power. It is through communion with the Lord that we are led to the pure waters that bring inner cleansing and transformation. If only we would stop our grumbling and fall to our knees in prayer. The Israelites had forgotten all that God had done for them in the past, and we are sometimes guilty of the same thing. They forgot how God suffered with them while they were in Egypt, and that it was his mercy and power that led them out of captivity. It is sad how present trials tend to erase our memories. Regardless of what God had previously done for them, the Israelites thought that he now left them to die in the wilderness.

After God allowed his Son to suffer and die for us, how could we ever think that he would abandon us. Moses had no power to cleanse the polluted water, but he knew the one who could perform the miracle. Like Moses, we must cry out to God for the water of divine grace that revives the soul and brings life. For those with faith, the solutions to life's problems are always close at hand.

SEEK THE KINGDOM FIRST

Luke 12:22–31

> Then Jesus said to his disciples: "Therefore I tell you, do not worry about your life, what you will eat; or about your body, what you will wear. Life is more than food, and the body more than clothes. Consider the ravens: They do not sow or reap, they have no storeroom or barn; yet God feeds them. And how much more valuable are you than birds! Who of you by worrying can add a single hour to his life? Since you cannot do this very little thing, why do you worry about the rest? Consider how the lilies grow. They do not labor or spin. Yet I tell you, not even Solomon in all his splendor was dressed like one of these. If that is how God clothes the grass of the field, which is here today, and tomorrow is thrown into the fire, how much more will he clothe you, O you of little faith! And do not set your heart on what you will eat or drink; do not worry about it. For the pagan world runs after all such things, and your Father knows that you need them. But seek his kingdom, and these things will be given to you as well."

Prior to this discourse, Jesus told the parable of the Rich Fool, in which he exposed the sin and folly of covetousness. In this lesson he reveals how people needlessly worry about their personal needs. Jesus points out that life is far more than the physical body and the things of this world. In other words, that which is not eternal will be eternally lost. What we accumulate in this life cannot compare to the soul's salvation and our eternal future. We get so caught up in the present, planning for our earthly future, that we give little thought to our spiritual lives and what is eternally important. Jesus stresses that we should think about the brevity and uncertainty of this life and look to God and his kingdom. He said if God takes care of nature, which is temporary and lacks a soul, then why would he not take care of us? According to Jesus, the Father knows our needs even before we come to him in prayer. Although we are God's children, we often drink from the well of secularism, rather than the living water that is found in Jesus Christ. How often do we go to God in prayer or meditate upon his living Word? Jesus once spoke to a Samaritan woman who was at Jacob's well. He told her that if she knew who she was talking to, she would ask him for living water. In her response, the woman wanted to know where she could get this water. Like many people, her thoughts were on the world, instead of on her spiritual needs.

The apostle Paul reminds us that salvation is not a once and done situation. Rather, it is a daily walk with God in which we offer up every room of our house. Jesus compares our relationship with him to a marriage, which suggests spiritual intimacy. It speaks to a relationship that is rooted in love, trust, and commitment, through all of life's difficulties. When Jesus Christ is first in our life, everything else falls into place, including our daily needs.

To seek the kingdom of God is to walk with Jesus Christ every day, laying our concerns and burdens at the foot of the Cross, knowing that our Savior understands our anxieties and pain. In Jesus we have a high priest who walked in our footsteps and can identify with all of our feelings, as well as the struggles that we encounter. The world cannot address our deepest needs, nor can it give us the wisdom and guidance to improve our life. Only by seeking the kingdom of God will we be filled with empowering grace and experience fulfillment and purpose.

THE SEA OF FEAR

Mark 4:35–40

> That day when evening came, he said to his disciples, "Let us go over to the other side." Leaving the crowd behind, they took him along, just as he was, in the boat. There were also other boats with him. A furious squall came up, and the waves broke over the boat, so that it was nearly swamped. Jesus was in the stern, sleeping on a cushion. The disciples woke him and said to him, "Teacher, don't you care if we drown?" He got up, rebuked the wind and said to the waves, "Quiet! Be still!" Then the wind died down, and it was completely calm. He said to his disciples, "Why are you so afraid? Do you still have no faith?" They were terrified and asked each other, "Who is this? Even the wind and the waves obey him!"

The setting for this scripture is the Sea of Galilee, a lake that is thirteen miles long and seven miles wide. It is the world's lowest freshwater lake, being 680 feet below sea level. It is surrounded by large hills, and the wind sometimes funnels down, causing turbulent water. Jesus had been teaching a multitude that was gathered along the shoreline, and when he finished he asked his disciples to take him to the other side of the lake. He was apparently exhausted and quickly fell asleep in the stern of the boat, when a severe storm developed. It wasn't long before the boat took on water, and the disciples responded with fear. Realizing that the boat was in danger of sinking, they cried out to Jesus, thinking that he was unconcerned about what was happening. In his response, Jesus took control of the situation by rebuking the wind and calming the sea.

The disciples were both confused and astonished, and Jesus admonished them for their lack of faith.

When I first read this passage, I was reminded of a trip that I took to Israel. It was a tour with a small group of people, and we traveled throughout the country with a guide, who was both a history professor and a retired military officer in the Israeli army. He scheduled us to take an evening boat ride on the Sea of Galilee, and needless to say we were all excited. However, within fifteen minutes after leaving the port, a sudden storm developed, which caused our fifty-foot boat to be tossed around. The captain immediately responded by bringing us back to the dock. Obviously, this biblical event now has more meaning to me. Also, having served in the U.S. Navy, I am aware how quickly things can change at sea.

Our lives are like the open sea, with its currents pulling us in different directions. We have also experienced those sudden storms, when our boat is simply too small to stay afloat. When life strikes fear in us, I wonder how many people cry out to God in anger and mistrust, believing that he is asleep and unconcerned. Do we really believe that Jesus can calm our turbulent lives? Sometimes we forget that the passenger in our boat is the Son of God, the one who has promised to never leave or forsake us. This is Jesus, who was raised from the dead and has the power to sustain us through all of life's trials. The question is, do we trust in his promises? Are we willing to completely give our lives to him, especially during those dark hours?

John Wesley was an Anglican priest and scholar who methodically studied the Scriptures, but there was a time when he struggled with his faith. This was revealed in the fall of 1735, when he sailed across the Atlantic Ocean from England to the United States. He was on a missionary voyage to Native Americans and settlers in the state of Georgia. The ship was the *Simmonds*, which was a 250-ton vessel. On this voyage there were 112 Colonists and nineteen crew members. Twenty-six of the Colonists were Moravians from Germany. It was a two-month trip, which began on December 10. During the voyage there were three violent storms, the last of which threatened to sink the ship.

Wesley had already been impressed with the Moravians, for he saw in them a spiritual maturity that he lacked. During this last storm he carefully observed them to see if their faith was real. As the storm raged, and the waves came crashing over the ship, damaging the main sail, the Moravians were singing in a calm manner. John Wesley was amazed at this, for he found himself gripped in fear. On that voyage he discovered that faith is not simply praising God when the sea is calm, or calling upon him when tragedy strikes. He learned that people of faith trust God in all circumstances.

We are not promised a trouble-free life, but we are promised grace to get us through the trials. Jesus tells us to have courage, for he has overcome the world. Life contains many storms, but our Savior is willing to be a passenger in our boat. He wants us to find comfort and strength in his abiding presence. Wesley discovered that faith is not merely a word in the Christian vocabulary. Instead, it is a life given to the Lord, through both the good and difficult times.

ABIDING JOY

Habakkuk 3:17–19

> Though the fig tree does not bud, and there are no grapes on the vine, though the olive crop fails, and the fields produce no food, though there are no sheep in the pen and no cattle in the stalls, yet will I rejoice in the Lord. I will rejoice in God my Savior. The Sovereign Lord is my strength; he makes my feet like the feet of a deer; he enables me to go on the heights.

The prophet Habakkuk was commissioned to announce the Lord's intention to punish Judah through the Babylonian captivity, which took place in 605 B.C. This was during the time when Nebuchadnezzar took Daniel and others to Babylon. These verses reveal a warning as well as a spiritual testing. How would the Israelites respond to this severe trial? Would they still have faith in the Lord? Were they spiritually prepared for the trials that were on the horizon? The people had already fallen into idolatry and were in a weakened spiritual state. How would they now cope with God's punishment?

Although Habakkuk's words relate to his own response to God's judgment, they were communicated to make the people look at themselves. When the land was invaded, their crops destroyed and livestock stolen, would they still trust God and be able to give him praise? This probing question forced the Jews to examine their spiritual lives and commitment to God. It also speaks to us, for no one is exempt from those times when everything seems to be falling apart, leaving us with a sense of hopelessness. Habakkuk was trying to assure the people that even when all seems lost, they could rejoice in God's abiding presence. He wanted them to know that their joy was rooted in a divine peace that circumstances cannot destroy. It is a joy that can be likened to the deep settled waters of the ocean that are not disturbed by turbulent weather. The joy that Habakkuk is alluding to comes when we rest our weary and troubled souls in the Lord. The prophet said, "I will rejoice in God my Savior. The Sovereign Lord is my strength; he makes my feet like the feet of a deer; he enables me to go on the heights."

It is God who is the life force of creation, and he alone can restore the soul and give us joy. Regardless of what happens in life, those who trust the Lord experience divine heights. If our joy were dependent upon this world, we would certainly be in trouble. Ours is a joy that is independent of life's tragedies and sorrows. I often think of Job, whose suffering was beyond our comprehension. He lost his possessions, family, health, and respect. Even his wife told him to curse God for what happened to him. But Job continued to love and trust the Lord through all his loss and pain. Even when he believed that God was punishing him unjustly, he still vowed his faith and love.

Just as God was always with Job, Habakkuk told the Israelites that the Lord would never leave them. They were about to meet the enemy, and the prophet was concerned how this would impact upon their spiritual life. When we meet the enemy, what is our response to the Lord? Whether it is the enemy of illness, fractured relationships, financial stress, or a deep personal loss, do we still experience God's presence? Is our joy dependent upon circumstances, or is it found in the Lord's promise of his abiding presence?

THE SKEPTIC

John 1:43–51

> The next day Jesus decided to leave for Galilee. Finding Philip, he said to him, "Follow me." Philip, like Andrew and Peter, was from the town of Bethsaida. Philip found Nathanael and told him, "We have found the one Moses wrote about in the Law, and about whom the prophets also wrote—Jesus of Nazareth, the son of Joseph." "Nazareth! Can anything good come from there?" Nathanael asked. "Come and see," said Philip. When Jesus saw Nathanael approaching, he said of him, "Here is a true Israelite, in whom there is nothing false." "How do you know me?" Nathanael asked. Jesus answered, "I saw you while you were still under the fig tree before Philip called you." Then Nathanael declared, "Rabbi, you are the Son of God; you are the King of Israel." Jesus said, "You believe because I told you I saw you under the fig tree. You shall see greater things than that." He then added, "I tell you the truth, you shall see heaven open, and the angels of God ascending and descending upon the Son of Man."

Nathanael was a skeptic, who could not believe that Jesus was the Messiah promised by the prophets. After all, how could God's Anointed One come from such an insignificant town. Nazareth was not only a small town, but it was known for its proverbial wickedness. So, who could blame Nathanael for his skepticism? Didn't he have reasons for doubt, and was therefore justified in his judgment of Jesus? This Jesus was a carpenter's son, who grew up amongst the people in a small village. How could the Messiah, sent by God to save the people, be an ordinary person? Nathanael would have to see something unusual or spectacular to believe that Jesus was the one promised by the Lord.

Nathanael was a skeptic, who made a judgment without objectivity or analysis. He came to a conclusion without even considering Jesus' identity. It was only when Jesus revealed a certain power that Nathanael changed his mind. This is the problem with those who refuse to allow the words of Christ to speak to their heart. They don't come close enough to experience his love and transforming power. Instead, they make a quick judgment based upon human reasoning. If one's mind is set, it matters little whether something is true. It is amazing that some individuals who make these snap judgments are educated professionals. So many people give praise to entertainers, athletes, and other high-profile people, but they refuse to consider Jesus as someone who can change their life.

Satan encourages us to look to the world for both answers and a fulfilled and happy life. After all, how can anything good come from Nazareth? How can faith in a carpenter's son save anyone? Isaiah's prophetic words have proven true, when he said, "Who has believed our message?" We live in a world that emphasizes the senses and the outer life. We are a society that is entrenched in human pride, materialism, and the spectacular, with little thought given to spiritual realities. In a sense, this was Nathanael's problem, for he was expecting a Messiah who would manifest political and royal charisma and power. But Jesus saw potential in Nathanael, just as he sees potential in everyone who will come close enough to receive his love and power. As Jesus promised Nathanael, he also tells us that our faith will enable us to experience great things from God.

MAKING COMPARISONS

Mark 2:18–20

> Now John's disciples and the Pharisees were fasting. Some people came and asked Jesus, "How is it that John's disciples and the disciples of the Pharisees are fasting, but yours are not?" Jesus answered, "How can the guests of the bridegroom fast while he is with them? They cannot, so long as they have him with them. But the time will come when the bridegroom will be taken from them, and on that day they will fast."

The question that Jesus was asked seems to be appropriate, at least on the surface. However, in reality it reflects a defensive attitude. Jesus was always questioned by the religious leaders of his day. In fact, prior to this particular question, he was asked why he ate with sinners. On another occasion he was asked why his disciples picked grain on the Sabbath. It appears that the legalism of these leaders clouded their understanding of God's truth. They simply could not understand why Jesus always bent the rules, which, of course, were written by them.

As we examine the Church, we continue to find believers making similar comparisons. This is seen on every level, both between laity and clergy. It is found within every congregation and also between denominations. There are churches that profess to have all the answers, even believing that they are the only way to salvation. Somehow, a faith relationship with Jesus Christ is not mentioned. We must remember that the kingdom of God is within each of us. It is a spiritual reality that is not dependent upon organizational and ritualistic rules.

The comparisons and judging that takes place amongst Christians is not only a poor witness, but it destroys the true meaning of the gospel. People of other religions cannot understand how the followers of Christ can be so divisive and engaged in continuous conflict. What often begins with believers asking questions of one another and making comparisons, leads to harsh judgments and accusations. Although it is natural to recognize the differences between individuals and groups, it is sinful to communicate abrasive attitudes.

Over the years, I have participated in a variety of faith and worship practices. Even within denominations there are significant differences. Some congregations are very conservative, while others are liberal and less orthodox. I have experienced charismatic services as well as silent forms of worship that focus upon meditation. Rather than the format of worship, it is the attitude of the heart that God examines. Our spiritual life incorporates many factors, including religious affiliation, culture, and congregational traditions. All of these factors, combined with changing times and different interpretations of scripture, define a particular group. But regardless of these differences, being a Christian is to walk in the love and forgiveness of Jesus. It is to grow in his image of humility and self-sacrifice, and looking for the good in other people. This requires that we look within, rather than making comparisons and judgments that lead to sinful thoughts and actions.

Four

COMPASSION

A COMPASSIONATE PRESENCE

Matthew 9:35–38

> Jesus went through all the towns and villages, teaching in their synagogues, preaching the good news of the kingdom and healing every disease and sickness. When he saw the crowds, he had compassion on them, because they were harassed and helpless, like sheep without a shepherd.

After a long tour of preaching and teaching, Jesus became deeply moved by the hopeless state of the people. He saw that they were confused and helpless, without a spiritual guide. The religious leaders were primarily concerned about themselves, not the common people. Jesus believed that many individuals would respond to the gospel if there were enough messengers; therefore, he prepared his disciples to share in his ministry of compassion. In fact, he even asked them to pray for more workers who would answer his call to the lost and dying.

What does it mean to answer the call of Jesus Christ? Have you ever taken the time to think about this? Over the centuries many of God's servants have pondered this question. Dietrich Bonhoeffer, the Lutheran pastor who stood up against Hitler and the Third Reich, was one such person. After much prayer and an agonizing spirit, Bonhoeffer became active in the plot to assassinate Hitler, and it cost him his life. It was Bonhoeffer's compassion for humanity and his understanding of the Scriptures that led him to this action. Even when in prison awaiting execution, he was a compassionate presence to the other inmates who were incarcerated.

Being a Christian is a life that is offered up to the Lord. It is living the sacrificial life of Jesus, which includes serving others in the spirit of love. But regardless of how we define our life in Christ, we must conclude that Christianity is a compassionate presence in the world. Those who have internalized the love of Jesus Christ see life and people through his eyes. We are compassionate toward others because it is our natural response. Instead of simply feeling a sense of obligation, we have a burden for all people in need. As the body of Christ, we share the nature and mission of Jesus.

Most people want their lives to have meaning. We have a desire to leave our footprints in the sands of time. I learned a long time ago that many people would rather see a sermon than hear one. When we answer the call of Jesus, we truly give of ourselves, leaving a lasting presence in the world. When we pray for the heart and mind of Jesus, enabling us to be a compassionate presence, we bring God's love into concrete forms. This is a recycling love, for it continues through those who have received it from us.

Jesus teaches us that whatever we do for the least of his children, we do it for him. By sharing our Savior's burden for humanity, we are driven to meet people where they are in life. This became a stark reality for me while serving as a state prison chaplain. In 1995 I was the chaplain for Pennsylvania's first execution in thirty-three years. After spending seven hours with a death row inmate, sharing our lives and spiritual journeys, he was taken into the execution room and prepared for the lethal injection. But just before this occurred, he informed me that my presence made a difference during the last seven hours of his life. More than anything else, it is a caring presence that speaks to the pain of others. Christians are disciples of compassion and ministers of reconciliation. Like Jesus, we must be weak with the weak, vulnerable with the vulnerable, and powerless with the powerless. The Lord wants us to place ourselves in another's position, regardless of who they are or what they have done.

When examining the life and ministry of Jesus we find that he was alert to the suffering that was around him, and he reached out in concrete ways. All situations were urgent to Christ, and there were no barriers that he did not cross. He was truly a servant to the world that he came to save, rejecting all manner of worldly acclaim. Sometimes we forget what it means to be a disciple of Jesus. As we get caught up in our daily routines, the focus is upon ourselves, with little thought given to the needs around us. The Church finds itself in the same situation. Rather than being the hospital that it is called to be, it sometimes slays its wounded. Instead of nurturing individuals who are emotionally and spiritually sick, it often pulls the plug on them. Everyone must examine their heart and the life that it reflects. Are we walking in the footsteps of our Savior? Are we really a compassionate presence to all people?

THE CALL FOR MERCY

Matthew 9:10–13

> Jesus saw a man named Matthew sitting at the tax collector's booth. "Follow me," he told him, and Matthew got up and followed him. While Jesus was having dinner at Matthew's house, many tax collectors and sinners came and ate with him and his disciples. When the Pharisees saw this, they asked his disciples, "Why does your teacher eat with tax collectors and sinners?" On hearing this Jesus said, "It is not the healthy who need a doctor, but the sick. But go and learn what this means: 'I desire mercy, not sacrifice.' For I have not come to call the righteous, but sinners."

The Pharisees were shocked that Jesus, who claimed to be sent by God, would associate himself with unclean sinners. In his response to these religious leaders, Jesus said that he came as a physician for the sick. To clarify who the sick were, he added that he came for sinners, not the righteous. This was a double-edged sword, for the Pharisees knew that regardless of their education and high position, they were still sinners before God. In a manner that would challenge their thinking, Jesus exposed their sins and their need for grace. Therefore, just as they needed mercy, God required them to show mercy to others.

On another occasion, Jesus told a story that highlights God's mercy and his command that we follow his example. It is about a servant who was in debt to his master. Because this man had no means to pay his debt, the master was going to have him jailed and sell all his possessions. But the servant begged the master for undeserved mercy, and surprisingly the master canceled everything that was owed. This, however, is not the end of the story, for this same servant had a fellow worker who was in debt to him and also asking for mercy. Not only was mercy not given, but the debtor was assaulted and thrown into jail. When the master was told what occurred, he was furious and sent the unmerciful servant to jail until his debt was paid in full. Jesus warned his listeners that this is how the Father will respond to those who refuse to be merciful toward others.

We are called to make a difference, and this means sacrificial involvement in the lives of people. Jesus has commissioned us to reach down and touch the hurting and the needy. Following the example of Christ, we are in the business of transforming and restoring broken lives. Like the Good Samaritan, the true Christian does not use a person's credentials as a criterion in deciding whether to show mercy. Jesus teaches that everyone is our neighbor, and no human need is beyond our concern and ministry. Our mission is to dispense mercy in a world that is crying out for help. Just as there are no limits on forgiving others, we must not set limits on our love. Our lasting legacy is the mercy that we show others, for it continues through the lives of those who receive it.

Rather than stilted rituals and mechanical forms of worship, God wants hearts that have been transformed through the power of his Spirit. Our sacrifices are the lives that we offer up to the Lord on a daily basis, and this includes being a servant of mercy to the forgotten segments of society. What makes us Christians is our participation in the pain that God feels for all who suffer. The question is, are we willing to walk where few people desire to go? To walk with Christ is a journey that takes us out of our comfort zones and into the real world.

Five

DIVINE GUIDANCE

TEACH US HOW TO PRAY

Luke 11:1–4

> One day Jesus was praying in a certain place. When he finished, one of his disciples said to him, "Lord, teach us how to pray, just as John taught his disciples." He said to them, "When you pray, say: Father, hallowed be your name, your kingdom come. Give us each day our daily bread. Forgive us our sins, for we also forgive everyone who sins against us. And lead us not into temptation."

When the disciples observed Jesus praying, they were deeply moved. Apparently, they never saw anyone pray with such a humble and intense spirit. In a sense, they experienced Jesus' faith and love for the Father. No wonder they asked him to teach them how to pray. After all, if John the Baptist shared insights with his followers, why would Jesus not do the same. Surely the apostles had prayed before, but there was something different about the manner in which Jesus approached God.

Jesus' disciples were given an example of prayer that emphasized the holiness of God. It also taught them the importance of trusting the Lord and the need to pray for God's earthly kingdom. In addition, they were to come to God for the forgiveness of their sins, while at the same time forgiving others of their trespasses. This brief example of prayer concluded by stressing the power of temptation in one's life. Jesus repeatedly spoke about the many influences and temptations that his followers would face, and how their submission to sin would lead them down a destructive path. The disciples needed to realize the weakness of the flesh, and their need to be rooted in faith and prayer.

Prayer is an expression of the heart for the things of God, and this is what the apostles saw as they watched Jesus pray. Deep within the heart of every person is the necessity for prayer, because within all of us is the need for God. Prayer is the cry of a child for its heavenly Father. But we must come to God in faith, trusting in his providence and will. It is our faith in Jesus Christ that brings us into God's realm, where he hears our voice. As we persistently pray for the Lord's will, we are assured of the Creator's presence in our daily activities.

Jesus came to the Father in faith and obedience, with the simplicity of a child. He came with his concerns and pain, praying for sustaining grace. This is how we are to approach the Lord, allowing the Holy Spirit to interpret what is inexpressible. The power is not centered in our words, but rather in the feelings that emanate from the heart. As we honestly search our inner life, we become one with God in nature and purpose.

Do we have this depth of spirituality, trusting in the Lord for our daily and future needs? Are we obedient to God's requirement that we forgive other people? Also, does our prayer life reflect God's command to pray for the salvation of souls? And finally, are we continuously praying for the power to resist temptation and evil, knowing that life is a perpetual battle between good and evil? When we pray in earnest, seeking the gifts of God, we will receive divine grace according to God's will.

PROMISE OF THE HOLY SPIRIT

John 15:26; Acts 1:8; Hebrews 2:3, 4

> When the Counselor comes, whom I will send to you from the Father, the Spirit of truth who goes out from the Father, he will testify about me.
>   You will receive power when the Holy Spirit comes on you, and you will be my witnesses in Jerusalem, and in all Judea and Samaria, and to the ends of the earth.
>   How shall we escape if we ignore such a great salvation? This salvation, which was first announced by the Lord, was confirmed to us by those who heard him. God also testified to it by signs, wonders and various miracles, and by gifts of the Holy Spirit distributed according to his will.

Jesus did not want his disciples going into the world until they received the Holy Spirit. He told them to stay in Jerusalem, where they would be clothed with power from God. On Pentecost, the Holy Spirit came as a mighty rushing wind, equipping the apostles to share the gospel message in the languages of the different regions. When the apostles prayed, that with boldness they might speak the Word of the Lord, the place where they were meeting was shaken, and they were filled with the Holy Spirit.

Paul stresses that our struggle is against the powers of darkness that seek to destroy the work of God within us. Apart from the indwelling Spirit we are simply too weak and vulnerable to stand firm against evil. We are in the grip of a spiritual battle that is often subtle, and this makes us susceptible to temptation and sin. Elisha saw a power in Elijah that he knew was necessary in order to stand firm against evil and to do the Lord's work. While power for many people is synonymous with wealth and worldly position, for the Christian it is found in the Spirit of God. The Church without the Holy Spirit is like a wax museum with lifeless bodies. There is no inspiration, excitement, joy, power, or vision. John Wesley said, "Give me twelve people who are filled with the Holy Spirit, and we will change the world for Jesus Christ." The Church needs people on their knees, praying that God's Spirit would consume their lives. When we receive the Holy Spirit we become recipients of God's all-consuming power and fortitude. This is the strength that prepares us for spiritual warfare.

To receive the Holy Spirit the conditions must be right. First, we must acknowledge our need for God's indwelling presence. This gives us the desire and initiative to take the necessary step, which begins with a penitent heart. Although people often take this first step, they succumb to the world's distractions and influences. What starts out as God's leading with personal potential is soon swallowed up by human pride and secularism. Rather than prayerfully seeking the Lord and faithfully waiting upon his guidance and power, people set the agenda and the timetable. We must frequently examine our lives and ask the probing questions: Is the Holy Spirit living and moving in us? Is there a daily surrender of our lives? And finally, is God's mighty rushing wind reaching others through us?

THE TRUE MANNA

John 6:47–51

> I tell you the truth, he who believes has everlasting life. I am the bread of life. Your forefathers ate the manna in the desert, yet they died. But here is the bread that comes down from heaven. If a man eats of this bread, he will live forever. This bread is my flesh, which I will give for the life of the world.

God provided the Israelites with a miraculous food, which they found on the ground during their wanderings in the desert. It appeared every morning, except on the Sabbath. It came in the form of a small round seed and was prepared for food by grinding and baking. The manna gave the people the life-sustaining food that they desperately needed. The Scriptures reveal that the whole nation subsisted on this food throughout their wilderness travels.

In this lesson, Jesus compares himself to the manna that kept the Israelites alive in their harsh environment. As the Father sent down manna to sustain physical life, Jesus, as the bread who came down from heaven, offers us everlasting life. The Israelites were about to perish in the wilderness, unless God miraculously interceded to save them. The people were starving and had to trust in God's love and care. There was no way that they could save themselves in such an arid place. Just as they were totally dependent upon divine intercession for their physical sustenance, our spiritual life is contingent upon the grace that flows through the sacrificial life of Jesus Christ. It was God's love that sent manna to the people, and this same love has given us the Bread of Life. The manna from heaven satisfied the physical hunger of the Israelites, and the living bread in Jesus meets our spiritual needs.

The world cannot satisfy the hunger and pain that accompanies living in sin. No amount of wealth or earthly power can bring forgiveness and feed the soul. But like the manna in the desert, which was within reach of every person, the life of Jesus Christ is available to everyone who steps out in repentance and faith. If the Israelites had refused to eat the manna they would have died, and we find the same situation for those who refuse to partake of the life that is in Jesus.

We must continuously strive to develop a closer relationship with the Lord. Our objective is to feed upon Jesus through increased faith and understanding. We are to internalize his teachings and promises, allowing the Holy Spirit to be our guide through life. To feed upon Jesus is to assume his nature and purpose. It is to possess his humility and to experience life and relationships through his love and wisdom. The apostle Paul told fellow believers that it was not he who lived, but rather Christ living in him. This is a powerful insight for those who seek the Christian life. What is the desire of our hearts? To become one with the Savior requires that we receive the manna that he offers.

CLEANSING THE TEMPLE

John 2:13–19

> When it was almost time for Passover, Jesus went up to Jerusalem. In the temple courts he found men selling cattle, sheep and doves, and others sitting at tables

exchanging money. So he made a whip out of cords, and drove all from the temple area, both sheep and cattle; he scattered the coins of the money changers and overturned their tables. To those who sold doves he said, "Get these out of here! How dare you turn my Father's house into a market." His disciples remembered that it is written: "Zeal for your house will consume me." The Jews demanded of him, "What miraculous sign can you show us to prove your authority to do all this?" Jesus answered them, "Destroy this temple, and I will raise it again in three days."

There is a striking difference between the scene at the marriage in Cana of Galilee and this one at the temple in Jerusalem. At the wedding, Jesus was an invited guest who pleased the people. In the Jerusalem temple, Jesus was an uninvited stranger in his Father's house, whose display of anger and judgment shocked those in attendance, especially the religious leaders. The temple was where God chose to reveal his glory to the Israelites, but the people were more concerned about rituals and making money. As Jesus stated, it had become a common market, rather than a place for prayer and worship.

Jesus referred to his body as a temple, meaning that it is the sanctuary of the living God. He said, "Destroy this temple, and I will raise it again in three days." The apostle Paul understood our bodies to be the temple of the Holy Spirit. He wrote the Corinthians that they were to honor their bodies, both physically and spiritually. Paul taught that our bodies are to be a living example of disciplined holiness, that God might be revealed through us. More than temples of stone, the Lord desires living temples that will penetrate the world for him. Jesus promised his disciples the indwelling presence of the Holy Spirit, enabling them to be witnesses of God's forgiveness and transforming power.

It was worldliness that defiled the temple in Jerusalem. Rather than a holy sanctuary, it became a place where anything but holiness was found. Instead of a house of prayer, the temple was a marketplace for greed and profit. It was no longer a spiritual refuge where people could pray and experience the presence of God. Unfortunately, this secular pollution has also invaded the Church and the lives of Christians. Both congregations and individuals have blocked the movement of the Holy Spirit, who seeks to dwell within them.

What do we find when we examine our lives? Are we a pure sanctuary that enables people to see and experience the love and power of Christ? We spend so much time on outer appearances, and devote little time to the inner life. The Jerusalem temple was an architectural masterpiece that impressed those who came to worship. But the world of sin penetrated its courts, turning it into a storefront where profiteers and thieves gathered. As a result, it lost its spiritual life and purpose.

It is the Lord who created our temple, with its uniqueness and multifaceted abilities. He has given us a soul that we might commune with him and be recipients of his love and glory. Through the Holy Spirit, God offers us his life, allowing us to be his adopted children. He calls us to be spiritual beacons that draw people to his Son, whose sacrificial death has paved the way to salvation. As the body of Jesus Christ, we are to share in the divine nature and mission. What can compare to a life that shines for God? Let us honor God by not allowing anything to defile the temple that he has graciously given to us.

Six

THE GREAT COMMISSION

THE COMMISSION

John 20:21, 22

> Jesus said to his disciples, "Peace be with you! As the Father has sent me, I am sending you." And with that, he breathed on them and said, "Receive the Holy Spirit."

As Christians, we are the body of Jesus Christ sent into the world to continue our Savior's mission of spreading the gospel message. In his prayer to the Father, Jesus said, "As you have sent me into the world, I have sent them into the world. For them I sanctify myself, that they too may be truly sanctified." The apostle Paul reminds us that we are ambassadors for Jesus Christ, spiritually set apart for the work of the kingdom. This means that we are God's officials, appointed to represent our Lord and Savior. What an awesome responsibility!

Our God-given lives are not without responsibility and service. The Lord has shown us his love and mercy by forgiving our sins and giving us a new life in Jesus Christ. We are both recipients and witnesses of his love and power, and he has sent us into the world to share these truths with others. Jesus was sent by the Father to redeem the world through his ministry, sacrificial death, and resurrection from the dead. But his work is to continue through the ministries and living examples of those who walk in his teachings and have received the gift of the Holy Spirit. Like our Savior, we are sent to proclaim freedom to the prisoners and recovery of sight to the blind, to release the oppressed, and to proclaim the year of the Lord's favor. The mission that was given to Jesus is now our commission.

Jesus told Peter to leave his fishing boat to become a fisher of men. While we are not necessarily led to leave our homes or place of employment, we are called to be the salt of the earth, which means that wherever we are, our lives are to make a difference. Regardless of geography or position, our life is to reveal a spiritual purification that touches other people and leads them to Jesus Christ. May we never forget how the lives of the apostles changed the world by laying the foundation for the Church. Throughout history we have seen the continuing effects of individuals who have committed their lives to Christ and the gospel. Like the apostles who started their ministry in Jerusalem, our ministries begin at home, within our own family circle and communities.

Although the miracles of Christ confirmed his divinity and inspired the apostles, it was his words that spoke to their hearts and changed their lives. We have not seen Jesus in the flesh, but his love and teachings have pierced our hearts with truth, setting us free from the bondage of sin. Rather than a sense of obligation or duty, it is this divine love that compels us to reach out to the world.

In the physical absence of Jesus, we have been given his Spirit to teach, guide, and empower us for service. We leave our sinful past behind for a higher purpose, which includes the salvation of others. Like Peter and the other disciples, we are called to be fishers of humanity.

SENT INTO THE WORLD
Luke 10:1–11, 16, 17

> The Lord appointed seventy-two others and sent them two by two ahead of him to every town and place where he was about to go. He told them, "The harvest is plentiful, but the workers are few. Ask the Lord of the harvest, therefore, to send out workers into his harvest field. Go! I am sending you out like lambs among wolves. Do not take a purse or bag or sandals, and do not greet anyone on the road. When you enter a house, first say, 'Peace to this house.' If a man of peace is there, your peace will rest on him. If not, it will return to you. Stay in that house, eating and drinking whatever they give you, for the worker deserves his wages. Do not move around from house to house. When you enter a town and are welcomed, eat what is set before you. Heal the sick who are there, and tell them, 'The kingdom of God is near you.' But when you enter a town and

are not welcomed, go into its streets and say, 'Even the dust of your town that sticks to our feet, we wipe off against you.' He who listens to you listens to me; he who rejects you rejects me; but he who rejects me, rejects him who sent me." The seventy-two returned with joy and said, "Lord, even the demons submit to us in your name."

Only Luke records this mission that Jesus gave to disciples outside of his inner circle. It reveals that he commissioned individuals who were not his twelve apostles, sending them out to prepare the way for his ministry. As he did with John the Baptist, the Lord uses ordinary people to prepare the way for the gospel message. This is a tremendous responsibility, for what we communicate through word and example often determines how people will respond to the gospel.

As we noted, the seventy-two disciples were sent out in pairs. While there may have been more than one reason for this, it reveals the importance of teamwork within the context of evangelism. As the body of Christ, we are not only a priesthood of believers, but we are coworkers for the Lord. We are called to be united in the essentials of our faith, utilizing our gifts to bring the gospel to the lost. Whether our mission is to plow the ground or plant the seeds, the goal is to prepare human hearts for the message of forgiveness and reconciliation. Our Lord's work does not belong to a chosen few, but rather to everyone who professes to be a Christian. Jesus emphasizes that the harvest is plentiful; therefore, there is always the need for more workers. If a farmer's field is ready, but there are no workers, the crop is lost. This truth also has spiritual applications.

Jesus sent his disciples out as lambs in the midst of wolves. Although they were to be individuals of peace and love, they were not to be naive about those who would try to block their mission. In addition, Jesus told them to leave worldly possessions behind. He wanted them to step out in faith, trusting that their needs would be met. Just as they were to prepare the way for Jesus, the Holy Spirit would prepare the way for them. Their mission was not to be delayed by long greetings that lead to extended visits, for they had a lot of ground to cover. The commission was only to prepare the way for the Savior's preaching and teaching ministry.

Jesus gave these disciples his authority; therefore, those who rejected them also rejected him. We are also sent out to share the love of Christ, enabling every person to make a decision. We must never allow rejection to discourage us from serving the Lord, for whatever we do in Jesus' name will always bear fruit.

RESPONDING TO THE MESSAGE OF JESUS

Luke 4:16–20

> He went to Nazareth, where he had been brought up, and on the Sabbath day he went into the synagogue, as was his custom. And he stood up to read. The scroll of the prophet Isaiah was handed to him. Unrolling it, he found the place where it is written: "The Spirit of the Lord is on me, because he has anointed me to preach good news to the poor. He has sent me to proclaim freedom for the prisoners, and recovery of sight for the blind, to release the oppressed, to proclaim the year of the Lord's favor." Then he rolled up the scroll, gave it back to the attendant and sat down. The eyes of everyone in the synagogue were fastened on him, and he said to them, "Today, this scripture is fulfilled in your hearing."

Jesus began his public ministry after his intense battle with Satan in the wilderness. After this time of testing, he went to Nazareth where he grew up. As Jesus quickly learned, the home field is often the most barren, especially when a familiar face claims to be the fulfillment of prophecy. Our Savior's quote from the prophet Isaiah, and his assertion that the prophecy alluded to him, brought an angry response from the people. After all, this was the son of Joseph and Mary. How could he be the Messiah promised by God?

The first response to Jesus was positive, but when he confronted what the people were thinking, they became furious. Knowing that they wanted him to prove his claim through some type of miracle, Jesus said, "Surely you will quote this proverb to me: 'Physician, heal yourself! Do here in your home town what we have heard that you did in Capernaum.'" Jesus told them that no prophet is accepted in his hometown, and he used the prophets Elijah and Elisha as examples. This angered the people more, and they drove him out of town, with the intention of throwing him off a cliff.

This incident speaks to the Christian Church, for people love to hear spiritual rhetoric from a servant of the Lord. The problem often comes when they are convicted by the messenger's words. Sometimes there isn't much distance between admiration and hate, particularly when it involves God's servants. In this case, the distance was in a single truth that would have changed the lives of our Lord's listeners. Although Jesus left the people in the synagogue, his truth remains for all who will believe.

Jesus came to proclaim the age of God's grace, with the sacrifice of his life being the means of freedom for those imprisoned by sin. Unfortunately, many people today respond to Jesus' claim with the same indignation as of those during his earthly ministry. To be confronted by God in any manner can be discomforting, and in some cases it may even arouse anger. The world defines freedom as living the way one desires, but the freedom that brings inner peace and contentment is through Christ. Jesus was trying to open the minds of the people, but they refused to listen. To them, Jesus was just the son of Mary and Joseph. There was no way that he was going to convince them otherwise. They wanted to see powerful miracles, possibly a cosmic event. They failed to recognize that the greatest miracle is the changed heart and spiritual sight. Jesus is the only name under heaven by which we can be saved, but people continue to choose their own path, ultimately realizing that it leads to a destructive end.

PREPARING THE WAY

Mark 1:1–8

> The beginning of the gospel about Jesus Christ, the Son of God. It is written in Isaiah the prophet: "I will send my messenger ahead of you, who will prepare your way, a voice of one calling in the desert, 'Prepare the way for the Lord, make straight paths for him.'" And so John came, baptizing in the desert region and preaching a baptism of repentance for the forgiveness of sins. The whole Judean countryside and all the people of Jerusalem went out to him. Confessing their sins, they were baptized by him in the Jordan River. John wore clothing made of camel's hair, with a leather belt around his waist, and he ate locusts and wild honey. And this was his message: "After me will come one more powerful than I, the thongs of whose sandals I am not worthy to stoop down and untie. I baptize you with water, but he will baptize you with the Holy Spirit."

The prophet Isaiah foretold the ministry of someone who would precede Jesus and prepare the way for the gospel message. John the Baptist did this by making people aware of their sins and the need for repentance and reconciliation with God. The prophet Malachi also spoke about a messenger, who was to prepare a spiritual path that would bring salvation.

In biblical times it was customary for advancing armies to send soldiers ahead of them for different reasons. They were often sent to proclaim a message, remove obstructions, level hills, and even construct roads. John the Baptist was sent to remove the spiritual obstacles to the gospel, and the response of the people seems to indicate a level of success. John's ministry was to make people look at themselves and to realize their need for a Savior. His baptism of repentance for the forgiveness of sins was the prelude to a new life in Christ. His mission was to give Jesus a smooth road into the hearts of the people.

John's water baptism was symbolic of the inner cleansing that takes place through repentance. In other words, it was an outer sign of past sins being washed away through God's forgiveness. Today, when individuals are completely immersed in water, it not only represents inner cleansing but also the death of the old person and the resurrection of the new life in Christ. John's ministry, although important to one's spiritual renewal, was to be followed by the baptism of the Holy Spirit, which occurs when Jesus is received into our lives.

Like the preparations John made for the coming of Jesus, we are to make our own preparation for his promised return. But are we taking every opportunity to prepare ourselves through devotions, prayer, and worship? There is a tendency within everyone to put off until tomorrow what we should be doing today, and this is true with our spiritual development. The Scriptures repeatedly address the subject of personal preparation while awaiting the Second Advent of Christ. This is a theme that runs through our Savior's teachings and those of the apostles.

When we examine our lives we find that we are always preparing for something. In fact, from the time we are children we are engaged in preparations. Whether it is school lessons or retirement, we are constantly in a preparation mode. So, why is it such a struggle to prepare for that glorious appearing of Jesus, when he will return to judge the world and receive the faithful?

THE GOSPEL OF RECONCILIATION

II Corinthians 5:17–19

> If anyone is in Christ, he is a new creation; the old has gone, the new has come! All this is from God, who reconciled us to himself through Christ and gave us the ministry of reconciliation: that God was reconciling the world to himself in Christ, not counting men's sins against them. And he has committed to us the message of reconciliation.

In Michelangelo's famous painting we see two hands in close proximity to each other. The hand of man is relaxed, with the fingers bent. The hand of God, however, has the index finger erect and pointing toward man. This symbolic expression reveals the Lord taking the initiative to give us life. One may view this as part of the creation story, or it may be understood as God giving spiritual life through the forgiveness of sins. But regardless how we interpret this painting, the message of God's mercy is clear. The apostle Paul reminded the Colossians of the great sacrifice God made to bring us salvation.

He wrote that the Lord's grace is total, and the gospel is inclusive. But Paul also tells us that receiving this grace brings responsibility, which means sharing the truth that we have received.

Paul wrote that everyone has sinned and fallen short of the glory of God. The apostle John emphasized this message, saying that if we claim to be without sin we deceive ourselves and the truth is not in us. John Wesley preached that we are bent toward evil, and any good in us comes from the Lord. But the good news is that in Jesus Christ we can become new individuals, whose sole desire is to please and serve the Lord. Although there is no perfection in this life, we can live a righteous life, which includes bringing the ministry of reconciliation to others. The Lord took the initiative that brought us forgiveness and salvation, and now we are to lead the lost to the saving grace of Jesus Christ.

Jesus came to open our minds and hearts to the realities of life and death. Our ministry is not selective, nor is our love conditional. We are to follow the path of Jesus, who gave his life for all people. Like the example of the Good Samaritan, Christians do not make exceptions when it comes to human need. The Church is a hospital for the sick, and we are the emergency-room workers. Our objective is spiritual healing and the mending of broken lives. We are not called to be religious, but rather compassionate servants of the Lord.

Jesus saw potential in everyone, regardless of their past, and here lies the true meaning of discipleship. In Christ, we give up our power over others that we might become servants of the Cross. In opposition to what the world believes, Christians view every person as equally loved by God. The world says get all you can, but Jesus tells us to give all we can. I have learned that people would rather experience compassion than simply hear about it. This is particularly true with non-Christians, who question the sincerity and love of believers. Without the love of Christ in us, we cannot take part in the ministry of reconciliation, for love is the essence of God's call and our outreach.

A CHALLENGING MISSION

I Kings 17:7–15, 17–24

> Some time later the brook dried up because there had been no rain in the land. Then the word of the Lord came to Elijah, "Go at once to Zarephath of Sidon and stay there. I have commanded a widow in that place to supply you with food." So he went to Zarephath. When he came to the town gate, a widow was there gathering sticks. He called to her and asked, "Would you bring me a little

water in a jar so I may have a drink?" As she was going to get it, he called, "And bring me, please, a piece of bread." "As surely as the Lord your God lives," she replied, "I don't have any bread—only a handful of flour in a jar, and a little oil in a jug. I am gathering a few sticks to take home and make a meal for myself and my son, that we may eat it and die." Elijah said to her, "Don't be afraid. Go home and do as you have said. But first make a small cake of bread for me from what you have and bring it to me, and then make something for yourself and your son. For this is what the Lord, the God of Israel says: 'The jar of flour will not be used up, and the jug of oil will not run dry until the day the Lord gives rain on the land.'" She went away and did as Elijah had told her. So there was food every day for Elijah and for the woman and her family. Some time later the son of the woman who owned the house became ill. He grew worse and worse, and finally stopped breathing. She said to Elijah, "What do you have against me, man of God? Did you come to remind me of my sin and kill my son?" "Give me your son," Elijah replied. He took him from her arms, and carried him to the upper room where he was staying, and laid him on his bed. Then he cried out to the Lord, "O Lord my God, have you brought tragedy also upon this widow I am staying with, by causing her son to die?" Then he stretched himself out on the boy three times and cried to the Lord, "O Lord my God, let this boy's life return to him." The Lord heard Elijah's cry, and the boy's life returned to him, and he lived. Elijah picked up the child and carried him down from the room into the house. He gave him to his mother and said, "Look, your son is alive!" Then the woman said to Elijah, "Now I know that you are a man of God, and that the word of the Lord from your mouth is the truth."

Elijah was a prophet whose life reveals continuous challenges and trials. Even while staying with this widow, his visit was not without difficulties. The woman lived in poverty, with little food left for herself and her son, and she was not looking for an unemployed prophet to live with her. But it was the Lord who sent Elijah to her house, that he might have food to eat, as well as be a servant of divine mercy and power for the widow and her son. The Lord made it known to Elijah that the household food supply would miraculously be supplied until there was rain to water the crops.

We learn that the woman was a nonbeliever who was antagonistic toward Elijah's religion. If you noted, she referred to the Lord as Elijah's God. She also asked Elijah if he had come to remind her that she was a sinner, and whether he came to kill her ailing son. It is apparent that she possessed inner guilt, and Elijah's presence was a reminder of her spiritual state. However, it was God working through Elijah that continuously provided her with food. It was also Elijah, whom God used as a channel to bring her son back to life.

Although the miraculous supply of food did not change the widow's heart, the restoration of her son's life did. It led her to see Elijah as a man of God, who had come into her life to bring renewal and hope. Elijah's brief stay and mission was also necessary to revive his faith and purpose in life. Yes, the Lord works in mysterious ways, and his miracles never cease for those who are obedient.

THE BODY OF CHRIST

Ephesians 1:22, 23

> And God placed all things under his feet and appointed him to be head over everything for the Church, which is his body, the fullness of him who fills everything in every way.

Paul told the Christians in Ephesus that the Father has placed all things under the authority of his Son. These brief verses reveal a divine mystery that the Church is the fullness of Jesus Christ. This means that, in a spiritual sense, the Church is our Lord's body on earth. What a powerful truth and message of hope! Every believer is a member of the living and mystical body of the Savior. We are not only given the commission to spread the gospel, but each person is the manifestation of Jesus' love and forgiveness. Just as Jesus taught his disciples the great and wondrous truths of God, we are called to do the same. Paul wrote that we are baptized by one Spirit into one body. It is the Holy Spirit who joins all believers together, to share in the nature and mission of Jesus.

As the body of Christ we have different functions, but we are one and equal, with each member being dependent upon the other. Like a physical body needs all of it parts, every person is essential to the working of the Church. With Jesus being the head of the Church, we take our authority directly from his teachings. As the body is the servant of the head, we are servants of Jesus Christ, reaching out to all creation with his gospel message.

To be united with Christ aligns us with God's will, both in a personal sense and collectively as the Church. As individuals and congregations walk in the Word and pray for leading, the Lord's will unfolds in ways not otherwise possible. But doing God's will may bring suffering as we resist sin and confront evil. If persecution befell the Master, we can be assured that we will face trials relating to our Christian values and message. Sometimes these trials develop within our families and circle of friends. It is interesting how some people treat us when they learn of our commitment to Jesus Christ.

Regardless of what lies ahead of us, we share in the power and glory of God. Beginning with the apostles and throughout the history of the Church, we have seen how the persecution of God's people has served as a catalyst in building the kingdom. The Lord has given men and women the courage to stand up for truth and justice, and they have changed the course of history. Whether it was Mary, the mother of Jesus, Martin Luther, or John Wesley, the body of Christ has stood firm against evil.

To reflect upon the life of the Church is also to examine our own life. Are we, in every sense, part of Jesus' living body, or do we simply go through the motions? The body of Jesus Christ has purpose and vision. It is a body that lives in and for the gospel, and one that is committed to the Savior. To be a member of our Lord's body is a calling to serve all people, which may lead us down a path of sacrifice and suffering.

Seven

REPENTANCE

THE REPENTANT SINNER

Psalm 51:1–12, 17

> Have mercy on me, O God, according to your unfailing love; according to your great compassion, blot out my transgressions. Wash away all my iniquity, and cleanse me from my sin. For I know my transgressions, and my sin is always before me. Against you only have I sinned and done what is evil in your sight, so that you are proved right when you speak, and justified when you judge. Surely I have been a sinner since birth, sinful from the time my mother conceived me. Surely you desire truth in the inner parts, you teach me wisdom in the inmost place. Cleanse me with hyssop, and I will be clean; wash me, and I will be whiter than snow. Let me hear joy and gladness; let the bones you have crushed rejoice. Hide your face from my sins, and blot out all my iniquity. Create in me a pure heart, O God, and renew a steadfast spirit within me. Do not cast me from your presence or take your Holy Spirit from me. Restore to me the joy of your salvation, and grant me a willing spirit to sustain me. The sacrifices of God are a broken spirit, a broken and contrite heart.

This psalm, which was written by King David, is one of deep sorrow and remorse. It resulted from David's sin with Bathsheba, which led him to plot the death of her husband Uriah. If you recall, God sent his admonition for David's sins through the prophet Nathan. Some believe that this psalm was not simply a private confession, but also a public expression of guilt and penitence. Although we cannot be certain, we do know that David wanted the forgiveness of both God and the people.

In this penitential psalm, David pleads for the Lord's forgiveness, praying for complete cleansing and restoration. He also promises to praise God for his love, and to communicate that love to others. There is no hint of self-defense or rationalization for his sins. He cried out to God, "Against you only have I sinned, and done what is evil in your sight." David sinned against Bathsheba and her husband Uriah, as well as his own family and throne. He even sinned against himself and future generations. But he was acutely aware that all sin is against God. Since the Lord is the Creator of all life, every sin we commit is against him.

When people sin, there is a tendency to shift the blame. Adam laid blame on Eve, and Eve blamed the Serpent. In psychology this is called projection, for we are taking what rightfully belongs to us and projecting it elsewhere. But our personal guilt for sin cannot be placed upon another person. When children get into trouble, some parents are quick to blame the influences of their child's friends. We all know, however, that sins belong to those who commit them.

David prayed for mercy, for nothing but God's forgiveness could change his life. What sinner would ask for justice, rather than mercy? Knowing our guilt and helplessness, we must fall on our knees and plead for mercy from the highest court. David also wanted his sins and iniquities blotted out. After all, what if God kept a record of sins? Can you imagine the Lord keeping a ledger on all of our sins, including our thoughts, words, and deeds? King David could not live with uncovered sins, and neither can we.

In addition to God's mercy and having his sins erased, David asked God to remove his guilt and to cleanse his heart. He said, "Cleanse me with hyssop, and I shall be clean." The hyssop plant was sometimes used in ceremonial cleansing and to sprinkle the blood of a sacrifice. Like a spiritual bath, David wanted the cleansing of God's forgiving Spirit. He also wanted the Lord to restore the joy of his salvation, by providing the inner witness of the Spirit that he was reconciled with his Creator. David prayed, "Do not cast me from your presence, or take your Holy Spirit from me." He combined this petition with his desire to have a willing spirit that would seek God's will in all things. He knew that as Israel's leader, he needed the continuous presence of the Holy Spirit. The mere thought of the Spirit's absence in his life brought anxiety and fear.

When David finished his prayer he made a resolution that he would teach transgressors the Lord's way. He promised to lead others to the Lord for their forgiveness, cleansing, and renewal. In all of this he would give God the glory.

Verses fourteen and fifteen read, "My tongue will sing of your righteousness. O Lord open my lips, and my mouth will declare your praise." Those who learn things the hard way have something to communicate to others, and David promised to do that. When blessed by God, we are called to share those blessings with those around us. Like David, we are to be witnesses of how the Lord is working in our lives, and gratitude is the best motivator.

David was not content to simply offer the sacrifices required by the law. His sacrifice would be the offering up of his life. He was making a promise to rededicate himself to both God and the people. Repentance is not simply asking for forgiveness, but it is responding to God's love by turning our lives around. This includes sharing our Savior's concerns for all people, and reaching out with acts of love.

CALL TO REPENTANCE

Luke 24:44–48

> Jesus said to his disciples, "This is what I told you while I was still with you: Everything must be fulfilled that is written about me in the Law of Moses, the Prophets and the Psalms." Then he opened their minds so they could understand the Scriptures. He told them, "This is what is written: The Christ will suffer and rise from the dead on the third day, and repentance for forgiveness of sins will be preached in his name to all nations, beginning at Jerusalem. You are my witnesses of these things."

In these verses the risen Christ wanted his apostles to understand the Scriptures, that the writings in the Law, Prophets, and Psalms, all point to him. He also emphasized that the forgiveness of sins comes through repentance and faith in him. Therefore, Jesus directed his disciples to preach the message of repentance to all nations, beginning in Jerusalem. Jesus teaches that the path to salvation begins with a sorrowful heart that seeks forgiveness for past sins. It continues through a life that prayerfully walks a righteous path that is rooted in faith and commitment.

The word repentance is found over one hundred times in the Scriptures. It is a theme that runs through the Hebrew Bible and emphasized with the teachings of Jesus and the apostles. John the Baptist preached a message of repentance for the forgiveness of sins and, when Jesus began his ministry, repentance was central to the gospel. Without a repentant heart we cannot be reconciled with the Lord, for it is repentance that opens the door to a faith relationship with our Savior. God forgives everyone who truly comes to him with a penitent heart. Repentance leads to changed ideas and desires, resulting in a new person whose life is pleasing to God.

Repentance is a positive response to the conviction of the Holy Spirit. It is acting upon the voice of the conscience, which many people believe is the Spirit speaking to us. When King David committed adultery and plotted a death, he was overwhelmed with sorrow and guilt. He experienced the continuing pain of his guilt, and he cried out to the Lord in sorrow and shame. Although our sins affect others, they are always committed against God.

The Lord calls us to confess both known and unknown sins, and this leaves no room for dishonesty and pride. We are also to mend relationships when and where possible, which often means taking the initiative. As difficult as it may be, the Lord calls us to be at peace with all people. Repentance is not a onetime situation, but rather a daily walk in which there is a continuous self-examination. But people struggle when it comes to judging themselves in the light of our Savior's teachings and example. It is much easier to see the faults of others and not the sins in our own life.

The Scriptures reveal both individuals and nations coming to repentance. Joseph's brothers repented of their maltreatment of him, the Israelites for worshipping the gold calf, King Saul at the reproof of Samuel, the apostle Peter of his denial of Jesus, and the Ephesians repented under Paul's preaching. These are but a few examples found in the Bible. But the question remains, are we responding to the convictions of the Holy Spirit?

FORGETTING THE LORD

Hosea 11:1–5

> When Israel was a child, I loved him, and out of Egypt I called my son. But the more I called Israel, the further they went from me. They sacrificed to the Baals, and they burned incense to images. It was I who taught Ephraim to walk, taking them by the arms; but they did not realize it was I who healed them. I led them with cords of human kindness, with ties of love; I lifted the yoke from their neck and bent down to feed them. Will they not return to Egypt, and will not Assyria rule over them because they refuse to repent?

Through the prophet Hosea, God reminded Israel what he had done for them. He spoke about how his love brought them out of Egypt, that they might be healed both spiritually and physically. The Lord emphasized the care and protection he gave the people as they encountered life's trials. Like individuals and nations today, Israel had forgotten the many ways that God's grace sustained them. In fact, they not only forgot the Lord, but they worshipped idols.

For whatever reason, forgetting the Lord is willful. People cast God aside simply because they don't want a Lord and Master. If you look at life, especially our culture, you find numerous reasons for this reality. First, we cloud over and distort our basic needs, such as the need for love, forgiveness, and a spiritual life. Secondly, there is an emphasis upon the physical and secular. This, of course, speaks to pride, ego, and worldly power. People desire to be the masters of their destiny, trusting in their own wisdom. Next are the many competing interests that fill our lives. Whether activities or entertainment, the list of distractions is endless. There is also the denial of death and the afterlife, which means that there is no need for God. With the focus upon secularism, little thought is given to preparing for eternity.

God delivered Israel that they might be set free in every way, including the freedom to love and be his witnesses of holiness. The Lord said, "I taught the tribe of Ephraim how to walk, taking them by the arms." What a beautiful picture of divine Fatherhood! It reveals a heavenly Father whose love, strength, and protection overcomes our weaknesses, and who is grief-stricken over losing their child to destruction. I am reminded of Jesus' sorrow over Israel, when he said, "O Jerusalem, Jerusalem, you who killed the prophets and stoned those sent to you. How often I have longed to gather your children together, as a hen gathers her chicks under her wings, but you were not willing. Look, your house is left desolate."

The early-Church fathers encourage us to remember those dark hours without God, when we chose to walk alone. This advice is worth heeding, for everyone has experienced times when they tried to travel their own path without God's leading and grace. We recall the emptiness and destructiveness that accompanies self-centered thoughts and actions. Like Israel, we sometimes get lured away by pride and false wisdom, becoming blind to the Creator's plan for our lives. We also lose sight of the realities concerning the uncertainty and brevity of life. People seem determined to turn away from God to follow their own ruinous path. Let us not forget that whatever leads us away from the Lord becomes a destructive idol.

PRAYERS OF THE HEART

Psalm 25:1–11

> To you, O Lord, I lift up my soul; in you I trust, O my God. Do not let me be put to shame, nor let my enemies triumph over me. No one whose hope is in

you will ever be put to shame, but they will be put to shame who are treacherous without excuse. Show me your ways, O Lord, teach me your paths; guide me in your truth and teach me, for you are God my Savior, and my hope is in you all day long. Remember, O Lord, your great mercy and love, for they are from of old. Remember not the sins of my youth and my rebellious ways; according to your love remember me, for you are good, O Lord. Good and upright is the Lord; therefore he instructs sinners in his ways. He guides the humble in what is right and teaches them his way. All the ways of the Lord are loving and faithful for those who keep the demands of his covenant. For the sake of your name, O Lord, forgive my iniquity, though it is great.

In this psalm, King David reveals essential elements of prayer, including an honest and in-depth search of his soul. This is clearly expressed when he said, "To you, O Lord, I lift up my soul." With this prayer, David had every intention of searching out his heart and offering up his feelings and personal assessment to God. For better or worse, he brought his inner probe before the Lord, asking for God's understanding and mercy. In other words, he laid it all at the altar of divine grace, including his true feelings and sins, as well as his frustration and anger. As we find in many of his prayers, David was not holding anything back. Rather than a mechanical and superficial petition, it was a prayer of the heart that was brought before the one who searches the heart of every person. David shared with God everything that concerned him.

David's prayer speaks to our spiritual life because it addresses the manner in which we should approach the Lord. Do we pray with an open and honest heart, offering our souls up to God? Do we lay it all at the altar? What sense does it make to lift our voice to the Lord but not our heart? True prayer comes from an honest and humble heart, but how many people pray in this manner? We have a Savior who, in every way, identifies with the human condition and seeks to be involved in our lives. Jesus has experienced our emotions and pain, eternally carrying the scars of human suffering. This understanding, along with his divinity, gives Jesus the power of both advocacy and grace.

In David's prayer we also find the elements of faith and patience. He prayed, "In you I trust, O my God." This statement acknowledges God as the only one who could meet his needs. David recognized a King higher than himself, and he entrusted his life to him. Faith requires patience, and David's words manifest his steadfastness when he said, "My hope is in you all day long." The King James version reads, "On thee do I wait all day long." Patience is a problem for everyone, especially in a world of computerized messages and responses. We are a people accustomed to instant gratification, and this can be problematic when it comes to our spiritual life. How many of us patiently wait upon the Lord?

This psalm encourages us to open our hearts to God, knowing that he cares and will address our concerns and needs. As we share our deepest struggles, we will develop an intimacy with the Lord not previously known. We will also increase our trust and find it easier to patiently wait upon his wisdom, love, and grace. The power of prayer is found in an open and honest heart.

Eight

FACING TRIALS

REACTION TO AFFLICTION

Job 1:6–12

> One day the angels came to present themselves before the Lord, and Satan also came with them. The Lord said to Satan, "Where have you come from?" Satan answered the Lord, "From roaming through the earth and going back and forth in it." Then the Lord said to Satan, "Have you considered my servant Job? There is no one on earth like him; he is blameless and upright, a man who fears God and shuns evil." "Does Job fear God for nothing?" Satan replied. "Have you not put a hedge around him and his household and everything he has? You have blessed the work of his hands, so that his flocks and herds are spread throughout the land. But stretch out your hand and strike everything he has, and he will surely curse you to your face." The Lord said to Satan, "Very well, then, everything he has is in your hands, but on the man himself do not lay a finger."

The Book of Job is dated as one of the oldest writings in the Bible and, although the author is not certain, it appears that Job was a historical person. He was from the land of Uz, an area along the border between Palestine and Arabia. Tradition assigns a town called Huran as Job's home. The prophet Ezekiel associated him with both Noah and Daniel. The Bible speaks of Job as being a good man, which the Lord confirmed in his conversation with Satan. He was one who feared God and rejected all manners of evil.

But Satan told God that Job was only righteous because of the way he was treated, for he was a very wealthy man whom the Lord had blessed. The devil said that if everything were taken away from him, the story would be different. If this occurred, Satan said that Job would lose faith and curse God. To prove Job's faithfulness, the Lord allowed Satan to bring deep personal loss into Job's life. As a result, Job's livestock were killed, along with his workers and servants. Even his sons and daughters died in a windstorm. If that wasn't enough tragedy, Job was stricken with boils that caused him severe pain. To add to all of this misery, his wife told him to curse God. Although he felt undeserving of these trials and cursed the day he was born, Job did not curse the Lord. When things could not get worse, he fell to the ground in worship and said, "Naked I came from my mother's womb, and naked I will depart. The Lord gave and the Lord has taken away; may the name of the Lord be praised." In spite of all that happened to him, Job did not sin.

Whenever tragedy strikes, friends often come into the picture, giving their assessment of the situation. Job had such friends, two of whom said that his trials must be related to sin in his life, and they urged him to repent. A third "so called friend" actually told Job that God was not punishing him enough. It is interesting how some people have all the wrong answers to life's problems. There was a fourth friend, however, who told Job that God always brings forth justice in the end, which was a message that needed to be heard.

After hearing from his friends, Job took his case directly to God. He told God that he was not a sinner, even suggesting that the Lord was deliberately trying to find fault with him. He told God that the good he had done was being rewarded with evil, and he wanted an answer from God. Needless to say, Job received an answer, but it was not the one he expected. The Lord reprimanded him for questioning divine wisdom. In his response, God asked Job probing questions about the created order as well as life and death. Job quickly realized that all wisdom and power belongs to the Creator. He also learned that the Lord was with him during these horrible events, providing him with sustaining grace. When their conversation was completed, Job apologized to God, which led to the restoration of his health. We also learn that he received twice as much as he previously had, and that he lived a long life.

Job was not without questions, but he remained a man of faith and commitment. Even when he lost everything, Job refused to blame the Lord. It was only after his friends told him that he was being punished for sin that he questioned God. The Lord revealed his anger against Job's friends for their false assumptions and judgments. They were commanded to offer a burnt offering and told that Job would pray for them.

While there are many lessons in this story, the major theme relates to how we face affliction. When we are going through difficult times, do we blame God for our troubles, believing that he is the cause of our problems? Or, as Christians, do we think that we should be removed from life's trials? It is easy to have faith and give praise to God when all is going well, but how many people can offer up praise during times of suffering? Job was able to do this after losing everything. Like this righteous man, how many people would fall to their knees in worship and say, "Blessed be the name of the Lord?" Job made it clear that even if he were slain by God, he would still love him. When the Lord told Satan that there was no one on earth like Job, he knew that Job would be faithful in the most painful of circumstances. Do our lives reflect this same love and trust? When tragedy strikes, are we able to worship and praise God?

THE HOLINESS IMPERATIVE

Hebrews 12:14–18

> Make every effort to live in peace with all men and to be holy; without holiness no one will see the Lord. See to it that no one misses the grace of God and that no bitter root grows up to cause trouble and defile many. See that no one is sexually immoral, or is godless like Esau, who for a single meal sold his inheritance rights as the oldest son. Afterward, as you know, when he wanted to inherit this blessing, he was rejected. He could bring about no change of mind, though he sought the blessing with tears.

While many scholars attribute this letter to the apostle Paul, others disagree because it doesn't adhere to the writing style of his other epistles. It was written to Jewish Christians sometime around 66 A.D., primarily to encourage them at a time when they were tempted to forsake Jesus Christ. In Chapter 10 of Hebrews the writer speaks about the earlier days, when the people were strong in their faith.

There were Jews who had genuinely accepted the gospel message and the promises of Christ, but they were being subjected to severe trials. Along with their adversity came discouragement, and this led to a lack of faith. This plot has a familiar ring to it, for it's the story of so many people. The years may have passed, but life's trials continue to test a person's faith and staying power. The initial excitement of God's forgiveness and a new life often dissipate as daily pressures overwhelm people.

Why were these new Christians in trouble? Was it their desire to walk away from their newfound faith? Christians should have the power to weather life's storms and stay the course. Actually, the problem facing these Jewish converts is a familiar one. After their conversion, they did not strengthen their spiritual roots. Simply stated, they failed to move on to holiness, and this made them weak and vulnerable. Earlier in this letter, the writer exhorted the people to leave the elementary teachings about Christ and go on to maturity. It is spiritual maturity that enables us to confront life's storms. Had the Jewish Christians matured in their Christian walk, their tragedies would not have weakened their faith. Like people today who are spiritually stagnant, the Jews did not deepen their understanding and faith, and they were about to lose their eternal inheritance. As a warning, the writer used Esau as an example. As the oldest son, Esau sold his inheritance rights to his brother Jacob. He later lamented this decision, but his inheritance was lost. The Jewish Christians were about to lose their eternal inheritance, unless they regained their faith.

Holiness is God's imperative, for only spiritual growth and maturity will keep us strong in the Lord. We must realize that our initial act of faith is only the beginning of our journey with Jesus Christ. When a young person is confirmed in the Church, it is supposed to mark the beginning of their new life. Unfortunately, it is often the end of their church attendance and spiritual development. We find this same situation with adults, who take the first step of faith only to allow complacency, trials, and distractions to consume them. The Lord wants us to be a holy people, who are totally set apart for him. Have we responded to the call that takes us beyond the basic teachings of Christianity?

LESSONS FROM ELIJAH

I Kings 19:9, 10, 15, 16

> And the word of the Lord came to Elijah: "What are you doing here, Elijah?" He replied, "I have been very zealous for the Lord God Almighty. The Israelites have rejected your covenant, broken down your altars, and put your prophets to death with the sword. I am the only one left, and now they are trying to kill me too." The Lord said to him, "Go back the way you came, and go to the Desert of Damascus. When you get there, anoint Hazael king over Aram. Also, anoint Jehu son of Nimshi king over Israel, and anoint Elisha son of Shaphat from Abel Meholah to succeed you as prophet."

After his victory at Mount Carmel, Elijah had all the prophets of Baal killed, which resulted in Queen Jezebel vowing revenge. Realizing the threat, Elijah first went to Beersheba where he left his servant. He then journeyed into the wilderness to hide. But he became discouraged, and he prayed that the Lord would take his life. While asleep under a juniper tree an angel spoke to Elijah, telling him to get up and eat. When he awoke there was a bread cake baking on hot stones and a jar of water nearby. After he ate, he rested once more, but the angel of the Lord appeared to him a second time, telling him to eat again, that he needed strength for his trip to Mount Horeb in the Sinai desert. It was there where the Lord would speak to him. This was the place where God spoke to Moses, and now Elijah was to have a private conversation with his Creator.

The trip to Horeb lasted forty days, and when Elijah arrived he took refuge in a cave. It was at the cave's entrance that the Lord spoke to him, but only after an earthquake and displays of wind and fire. It was in a gentle whisper that God asked him why he was there. Elijah came to speak to the Lord about the threats on his life and how all the Israelites, except him, were lost to idol worship. He was living in fear and depression to such an extent that he wanted to end his work and life. He saw his prophetic office as fruitless, especially in light of the people's sins and their refusal to repent and return to the Lord.

Although Elijah's facts and reasoning were flawed, he was honest with his feelings. In love and understanding the Lord responded to his emotions and state of mind. He gave his prophet an assignment that did not require the dangers he previously encountered. Elijah was to go to the desert of Damascus, where he was to anoint Hazael king over Aram and Jehu as king over Israel. Then, what may have been a surprise, the Lord told him to anoint Elisha as his successor.

Elijah was a man of God, but the Lord knew that he could no longer function as a prophet. He had been on God's front line, giving his life for truth and justice. Like the apostle Paul, he fought the good fight and finished the race. It was now time to be in the background, serving God in other ways until he was taken home. This occurred in a dramatic way, for it is recorded that a chariot of fire appeared and took him up to heaven in a whirlwind, leaving Elisha to carry on his mission.

When we are discouraged, it is not necessary to flee or travel to the desert to speak to God. We only need to pray, and listen for the Lord's compassionate and gentle voice. As his faithful servants, we will be taken to a place for healing and renewal, where we will find rest until we are called home.

CHOOSING PRIORITIES

Luke 10:38–42

> As Jesus and his disciples were on their way, he came to a village where a woman named Martha opened her home to him. She had a sister called Mary, who sat

at the Lord's feet listening to what he said. But Martha was distracted by all the preparations that had to be made. She came to him and asked, "Lord, don't you care that my sister has left me to do the work by myself? Tell her to help me!" "Martha, Martha," the Lord answered, "you are worried and upset about many things, but only one thing is needed. Mary has chosen what is better, and it will not be taken away from her."

This is a timeless truth about priorities, and what is most important for our lives. In a sense, it is a lesson about life and death, for what we consider to be important in this life speaks to our eternal destiny. Martha and Mary were the sisters of Lazarus, whom Jesus had raised from the dead. Our Lord had become a close friend of the family, and his visits were a special time for them. This is probably why Martha was concerned that everything was in order, and why she was upset that her sister was not helping her. I am certain that most people can identify with this picture.

While Martha was running around making preparations, her sister Mary was intently listening to Jesus, who was speaking about the kingdom of God and spiritual matters. Mary, being engrossed in the conversation, forgot about her sister shouldering most of the work. This did not sit well with Martha, and she went to Jesus with the complaint. The fact that she did this reveals the extent of her frustration. With compassion for his dear friend, Jesus responded, saying, "Martha, Martha, you are upset about many things, but only one thing is needed. Mary has chosen what is better, and it will not be taken away from her." Jesus was telling Martha that the things of this life, while important, are temporary and not worth getting upset about. Instead, our priority should be our relationship with God and eternal life.

We live in a fast moving world, in which people spend more time working on their homes and in front of their computers than they do with developing their spiritual life. Like a magnet, it's a world that pulls us away from the Lord. Everything is important, except what really matters. In the first-century town of Bethany, there wasn't much going on; no amusement parks, movie theaters, or athletic fields. There wasn't even a shopping mall to occupy a person's time. But regardless of the culture and time in history, there are always choices and priorities to consider. Jesus wanted Martha to know where her priorities should be.

If you were told that you had a month to live, what would be your priority? The truth is that we may not even have a month to live. But if people realize the brevity and uncertainty of life, why do they continue down the wrong path? Our Lord's response to Martha speaks volumes, for it forces us to look at our priorities in life. In just a matter of seconds, Jesus brings us to the sudden realization that we must make changes in the way we think and how we spend our time. We should frequently examine our lives, making certain that we give adequate time to our spiritual development. We tend to be like Martha, worrying about things that are temporary. We are only here for a short while; therefore, it is crucial that our priorities be in order.

WHEN DEPRESSION COMES

Psalm 42:1–6

> As the deer pants for streams of water, so my soul pants for you, O God. My soul thirsts for God, for the living God. When can I go and meet with God? My tears have been my food day and night, while men say to me all day long, "Where is your God?" These things I remember as I pour out my soul: how I used to go with the multitude, leading the procession to the house of God, with shouts of joy and thanksgiving among the festive throng. Why are you downcast, O my soul? Why so disturbed within me? Put your hope in God, for I will yet praise him, my Savior and my God.

This psalm was written by King David during a time of anxiety and despair. It was when his son Absalon drove him into exile north of Palestine. David had to leave Jerusalem, the city that he loved. His life had fallen apart, and he longed to return to the past when he was able to lead the worshipers to God's house. When David wrote this psalm he was in a deep state of depression, and he cried out to the Lord from the depth of his soul.

Numerous people admit to having chronic depression, many of whom are well known, such as Winston Churchill, Ernest Hemingway, and Abraham Lincoln. The great preacher Charles Spurgeon claims to have often battled depression. In the Scriptures, Moses and Elijah certainly had their emotional struggles, and so did the prophets Jeremiah, Job, and Jonah. Many theologians believe that Jesus had times when the burdens of the world impacted upon his emotional state. Sometimes we forget that he shared in our humanity to the fullest extent. In this life there will be times when the most positive and hopeful individuals are brought down by the weight of certain situations and trials, and Christians are not excluded. There are numerous reasons why people experience depression, some of which can make a person vulnerable to other problems. King David certainly had reasons for his feelings, having lost everything that had meaning to him. His son Absalon wanted his power, and this started a series of painful events that ended in Absalon's death.

Because of David's many tragedies, people taunted him about his God. They wanted to know why God was allowing these things to happen. After all, David was a righteous man who praised the Lord before the people. These responses led David to question God about his circumstances. In verse nine he wrote, "I say to God my Rock, why have you forgotten me? Why must I go about mourning, oppressed by the enemy?" If you recall, in the Garden of Gethsemane, Jesus also questioned the Father about the suffering he was about to endure. He prayed, "My Father, if it is possible, may this cup be taken from me." This was followed by his acceptance of God's will.

David took his depression to the Lord, saying, "My soul thirsts for God, for the living God. When can I go and meet with God? My tears have been my food day and night." When we are in the valley of depression we sometimes have difficulty bringing our feelings to the Lord. Our emotions overwhelm us, and prayer becomes a struggle. This is a spiritual battle that we must overcome, for it is only our communion with God that brings inner peace and restores our soul. Regardless of the trials, David trusted in the Lord, and he tells us to do the same. He said, "Put your hope in God, for I will yet praise him."

A CRY FOR MERCY

Matthew 15:21–28

> Jesus withdrew to the region of Tyre and Sidon. A Canaanite woman from that vicinity came to him, crying out, "Lord, Son of David, have mercy on me! My daughter is suffering terribly from demon possession." Jesus did not answer a word. So his disciples came to him and urged him, "Send her away, for she keeps crying out after us." He answered, "I was sent only to the lost sheep of Israel." The woman came and knelt before him, "Lord, help me!" she said. He replied, "It is not right to take the children's bread and toss it to their dogs." "Yes, Lord," she said, "but even the dogs eat the crumbs that fall from the master's table." Then Jesus answered, "Woman, you have great faith! Your request is granted." And her daughter was healed from that very hour.

Matthew reports that a Canaanite woman came to Jesus in sadness and distress, seeking the healing of her daughter. The Canaanites were considered heathen and outcasts by the Jews, which meant that her coming to Jesus was an act of both desperation and faith. At first, Jesus did not respond to her plea. The disciples saw her as an intrusion and aggravation, and they let Jesus know how they felt. Then, what seems to be indifference, Jesus said to her, "I was sent only to the lost sheep of Israel. It is not right to take the children's bread and toss it to their dogs." But rather than this response being a lack of compassion, Jesus was putting the woman's faith to the test, and she passed with flying colors. "Yes, Lord," she said, "but even the dogs eat the crumbs that fall from their master's table." Jesus then answered, "Woman, you have great faith! Your request is granted." From that moment the woman's daughter was healed of her demon possession.

The Canaanite woman came to Jesus in humility and faith, knowing how the Jews felt about her race. But somehow she thought that Jesus was full of compassion and anointed with divine power. She came wanting Jesus to heal her daughter of demon possession; however, in her request she asked Jesus to have mercy on her. It wasn't only the daughter who needed God's grace, but also the mother who suffered because of the daughter's hopeless condition. The need was for an exorcism, but the results provided a channel for blessings beyond the woman's request. Can you imagine the woman's response, if she had known that her plea was made to the Son of God?

The world may be deaf to the cries of the needy, but the Lord responds to our suffering. Just as a mother listens during the night for the cries of her infant child, God is always waiting to respond to our pain. The disciples wanted Jesus to send her away because she was annoying them. Individuals so often respond in this manner, seeing the needs of others as an inconvenience or irritant. However, the woman approached Jesus with a broken spirit, taking her place with the undeserving. It was her humble and contrite spirit that opened the floodgates of mercy.

Though Jesus at first was silent and his disciples insensitive, the woman never stopped believing in the one to whom she was led. She looked to Jesus for the love and power that she needed. The world called her a dog, but Jesus called her a woman of great faith. Sometimes we forget that every person is God's child, and his grace is available to all who come to him in humility and faith. Even when there is silence, we must have faith and patiently wait upon the Lord. Our hope is in the wisdom and power of a holy and merciful God, who will never turn a deaf ear toward those who call out to him for mercy.

TRIALS THAT BRING MINISTRY

Acts 28:1–10

> Once safely on shore, we found out that the island was called Malta. The islanders showed us unusual kindness. They built a fire and welcomed us all because it was raining and cold. Paul gathered a pile of brushwood and, as he put it on the fire, a viper, driven out by the heat, fastened itself on his hand.

When the islanders saw the snake hanging from his hand, they said to each other, "This man must be a murderer; for though he escaped from the sea, justice had not allowed him to live." But Paul shook the snake off into the fire and suffered no ill effects. The people expected him to swell up or suddenly fall over dead, but after waiting a long time and seeing nothing unusual happen to him, they changed their minds and said he was a god. There was an estate nearby that belonged to Publius, the chief official of the island. He welcomed us to his home and for three days entertained us hospitably. His father was sick in bed, suffering from fever and dysentery. Paul went to see him and, after prayer, placed his hands on him and healed him. When this took place the rest of the sick on the island came and were cured. They honored us in many ways, and when we were ready to sail, they furnished us with the supplies we needed.

The apostle Paul had been arrested for preaching the gospel, and he was taken before Felix, the governor of Caesarea. This resulted in his imprisonment for two years. Felix was succeeded by Porcius Festus, who also heard Paul's case. It was before Festus that Paul appealed his case to Caesar. As a Roman citizen, he had the right to seek an appeal on his charges. But before the appeal occurred, Festus asked King Agrippa, who was the ruler of Palestine, to hear Paul's case. Agrippa permitted the appeal, and Paul and other prisoners were handed over to a centurion named Julius. They were placed aboard a ship and headed for Rome, where Paul's appeal was to take place.

While at sea, a wind of hurricane force threatened to sink the ship, and they ran aground on a sand bar off the island of Malta. During the storm an angel of the Lord appeared to Paul, telling him that every person would be spared. The soldiers had planned to kill the prisoners to prevent them from escaping, but the centurion prevented this. They were all able to reach the shore, where the islanders welcomed them and took care of their needs.

Some interesting things took place on the island that directly related to Paul. First, there was the trial at sea, and then Paul's life was in danger when the islanders thought he was a murderer. However, when he survived the snakebite, the people then believed that he was a god. With this matter being resolved, Paul was invited to the home of the island's chief official, where he was able to reveal God's glory. Who could have known that God's healing power would result from a tragedy at sea and a life-threatening situation on the island. When the islanders thought that Paul was a god, the door was open to share the gospel. Also, the miracles that Paul performed gave him the opportunity to direct the people to the Lord. Throughout his ministry, Paul used all of his trials to communicate the love and power of Jesus Christ.

No one goes through life looking for trials and suffering, but God can use every situation to speak to the hearts of people. The manner in which we weather life's storms can serve as a witness to God's presence in the world. Through the trials of this one apostle, God was able to manifest his miraculous power. Like Paul, we are called to turn our struggles into victories.

Nine

RESISTING TEMPTATION

ENEMIES OF THE CROSS

Philippians 3:16–21

> Let us live up to what we have already attained. Join with others in following my example, brothers, and take note of those who live according to the pattern we gave you. For as I have often told you before and now say again even with tears, many live as enemies of the cross of Christ. Their destiny is destruction, their god is their stomach, and their glory is in their shame. Their mind is on earthly things. But our citizenship is in heaven. And we eagerly await a Savior from there, the Lord Jesus Christ, who by the power that enables him to bring everything under his control, will transform our lowly bodies so that they will be like his glorious body.

In this letter Paul was urging believers to live holy lives. He did not want them to fall back into the sins of their past. In verse sixteen he wrote, "Let us live up to what we have already attained." This was a reminder that the people should live as the Christians that they had grown to be. Paul used himself and other mature Christians as examples, saying, "Join with others in following my example, and take note of those who live according to the pattern we gave you." It was important to Paul that people follow the humility, wisdom, and love of those who had surrendered their lives to Christ.

In verse eighteen Paul turns his thoughts to individuals who have already fallen back into sinful living. He wrote, "I have often told you before, and now say again even with tears, many live as enemies of the cross of Christ." What is

Paul's message here? Who are these enemies, and what makes them an enemy of the cross? To answer this question we need to understand that the cross of Jesus Christ reflects the depth of God's love and forgiveness for humanity. It is the sacrifice at Calvary that tells us how important every sinner is to the Lord. God's love for us is so deep that it brought suffering and death within the Godhead. The cross was, and continues to be, God's heart bleeding for a world in need of forgiving and saving grace. Therefore, to be an enemy of the cross is to be an enemy of God's sacrificial love. It is rejecting the sacrificial death of Christ that sets us free. The mere thought of this brought tears to the apostle Paul. Not only were people lost to sin and rejecting God's love, but they were injuring others by their poor example.

Paul states that the enemies of the Cross are controlled by sinful desires and appetites. Their god is the world, and they are only concerned about themselves. He wrote that such people glory in their shame, meaning that they glory in things that are shameful before God. Paul agonized over false disciples, whose hearts had never changed. He saw them as an obstacle to the gospel message and the work of the Church. They were a stumbling block for people who were seeking truth and a changed life.

Just as Paul challenged the Philippians, his words also speak to us. Have we received the transforming power of the Holy Spirit? Are we praying for the power to resist temptation and sin? Do we make every effort to live the teachings of Jesus, and are we growing in our Savior's image?

REMEMBER LOT'S WIFE

Luke 17:32–37

> Jesus said to his disciples, "Remember Lot's wife! Whoever tries to keep his life will lose it, and whoever loses his life will preserve it. I tell you, on that night two people will be in one bed; one will be taken and the other left. Two women will be grinding grain together; one will be taken and the other left." "Where Lord?" they asked. He replied, "Where there is a dead body, there the vultures will gather."

With these words, Jesus was speaking about his Second Coming and the judgment that will take place. He was communicating a warning that people be prepared by seeking the life of God. He told his disciples that they must never look back yearning the old life of sin. To emphasize this point he alluded to Lot's wife, who after leaving the sinful city of Sodom, looked back and became a pillar of salt. As the Lord cast his judgment upon the city, it was her hesitation to leave Sodom that led to her death. Jesus makes it clear that his return will be swift and without warning; therefore, we must be certain that our sinful past is behind us. The kingdom of God is twofold, for it is within the heart, and yet to be fulfilled with the return of Jesus Christ. This means that our hearts cannot be divided. In teaching the people, Jesus said that whoever sets their hand to the plow and looks back, is not fit for the kingdom of God.

The body of Lot's wife was not in the city, but her heart was there, and she perished even though she was the wife of a righteous man. Not only was Lot's wife married to a man of faith, but she was related to Abraham, who throughout the centuries has been our example of faith. We freely make our decisions, and everyone is responsible for their own life. Proximity to righteousness matters little, if the will is unwilling and the heart is not right before God. Lot's wife knew of the impending judgment, for there was a warning message from God. Although she made a move to leave Sodom, she was reluctant to put the past behind her. She, like many people, tried to have it both ways. As Jesus repeatedly teaches, sin is the refusal of the heart. The author of Hebrews wrote, "My righteous one will live by faith. And if he shrinks back, I will not be pleased with him. But we are not of those who shrink back and are destroyed, but of those who believe and are saved." He also wrote, "We must fix our eyes on Jesus, the author and finisher of our faith."

Jesus used the tragedy of Lot's wife to show us the plight of people who try to live in two worlds. Our Savior not only spoke of her death in a physical sense, but he emphasized her spiritual state. It was her refusal to follow God's path that led to her judgment. The call to follow Jesus allows no room for hesitation or yearning for the sinful past. The Scriptures tell us that the apostles left everything behind to follow Jesus. While this is obviously understood in a secular sense, the spiritual aspect of their calling and life cannot be denied. Do we understand what it means to leave our past behind us?

PETER'S DENIAL

Luke 22:54–62

> Then seizing him, they led him away and took him into the house of the high priest. Peter followed at a distance. But when they had kindled a fire in the middle of the courtyard and had sat down together, Peter sat down with them. A servant girl saw him seated there in the firelight. She looked closely at him and said, "This man was with him." But he denied it. "Woman, I don't know him," he said. A little later someone else saw him and said, "You also are one of

them." "Man, I am not!" Peter replied. About an hour later another asserted, "Certainly this fellow was with him, for he is a Galilean." Peter replied, "Man, I don't know what you are talking about." Just as he was speaking, the rooster crowed. The Lord turned and looked straight at Peter. Then Peter remembered the word the Lord had spoken to him: "Before the rooster crows today, you will disown me three times." And Peter went outside and wept bitterly.

Peter was forewarned that he would disown his Savior, but Jesus' words did not take root. Peter was confident that this would not occur, but fear for his life suddenly changed things. It was Peter who always revealed outer strength, and the one who promised never to forsake Jesus. But on three occasions after our Savior's arrest, he denied knowing Christ. The one who manifested leadership qualities and who appeared to possess unshakable faith was found cowering in fear. Even though he knew that Jesus was God's Messiah, he was unable to stand firm in his faith and commitment. At a time when he could have been a great witness, he crumbled under Satan's power.

What a clear and graphic lesson for those who profess an unyielding faith in Jesus Christ. So many people reveal spiritual strength when in God's sanctuary and in the fellowship of other Christians, but they succumb to the sinful influences of the world. Like the apostle Peter, people make professions and promises, but they sometimes fall prey to their weaknesses. They acknowledge Jesus as their Savior, but their spiritual immaturity does not provide the strength that is necessary to stand firm when tested. Peter told Jesus that he was ready to follow him to prison or death, but when the time came his own life was more important. Although he thought he was ready, the testing revealed otherwise.

When Jesus was arrested, Peter followed the arresting party at a distance. This was the time when he could have fulfilled his promise to follow Jesus to prison or death. But Peter discovered that faith goes much deeper than words, and that commitment leads to sacrifice. The world is full of people who profess Jesus as Savior, yet they follow at a distance, fearing that there will be some manner of sacrifice.

Following at a distance is not the surrender of one's life; therefore, there is little or no power to stand firm when confronted with temptation and trials. Peter certainly loved the Lord, but he was not prepared for the first challenge of his faith. Later, however, this great apostle martyred his life for Christ and the gospel. Because he felt unworthy to be crucified in the same manner as Jesus, he requested to be crucified upside down. According to tradition, his request was granted. Peter's life provides hope for everyone, for it emphasizes that our weaknesses are overcome by trusting in the Lord. Peter never again disowned Jesus, for his love and faith gave him the strength to live only for his Savior.

THE FALSE DISCIPLE

Mark 14:43–46

> Just as he was speaking, Judas, one of the Twelve, appeared. With him was a crowd armed with swords and clubs, sent from the chief priests, the teachers of the law, and the elders. Now the betrayer had arranged a signal with them: "The one I kiss is the man; arrest him and lead him away under guard." Going at once to Jesus, Judas said, "Rabbi!" and kissed him. Then the men seized Jesus and arrested him.

A false disciple is one who wears the cloak of Christianity but doesn't live the life. Judas Iscariot was a false disciple, who did not possess the heart of Jesus. But how could Judas betray the one who he came to know as a man of love and forgiveness? For almost three years he and the other disciples lived with Jesus, witnessing his authority over evil and his power to heal the sick and raise the dead. So, why did Judas betray Christ?

Biblical scholars have come up with a list of possible reasons why Judas would seek the demise of Jesus. Was Judas a false disciple from the beginning, sent by the religious leaders to plot the arrest of Jesus? If not, did something happen during his years with Jesus that changed him? Was Judas angered when he learned that our Savior was not seeking to overthrow the Roman government, or was it simply the thirty pieces of silver, which today is worth approximately fifteen dollars? Most students of scripture believe that Judas' reason related to politics. He wanted Jesus to lead an uprising against the Roman government that would restore the Jewish nation.

To think of oneself as a false disciple is difficult, and we tend to block such thoughts from our minds. In the field of psychology this is called repression or denial. We are quite gifted at coming up with excuses for our actions, or the lack of them. How many people will honestly examine their spiritual lives and their relationship with the Lord? Although society may view us in a positive light, it is God who searches the mind and heart. Countless individuals, including professing Christians, betray Jesus everyday with their thoughts, words, and actions.

Some of the ways that people betray Christ is through compromise. Rather than placing God first in their lives and standing firm against sin, they bend under temptation and the influences of others. The temptations of life are numerous, which means that awareness and discipline, combined with persistent and earnest prayer, are absolutes. Even the most mature Christians find themselves influenced by sin, thereby losing opportunities offered by the Lord.

We must prayerfully allow God to probe our lives for those areas that need to be changed. When doing this, we will find that our priorities are sometimes out of order, and that the time we give to God and spiritual development is very little. This speaks to who we are as well as who we are becoming. Jesus knows our weaknesses, and he warns us to seek God's kingdom first. When we do this, we will not only walk in righteousness, but our needs will also be met. Only when we live in Christ will we receive the fullness of God's blessings, which include the strength to stand firm in our commitment.

Ten

COMMITMENT

THE VINE AND BRANCHES

John 15:1–8

> Jesus said, "I am the true vine, and my Father is the gardener. He cuts off every branch in me that bears no fruit, while every branch that does bear fruit he trims clean, so that it will be even more fruitful. You are already clean because of the word I have spoken to you. Remain in me, and I will remain in you. No branch can bear fruit by itself; it must remain in the vine. Neither can you bear fruit unless you remain in me. I am the vine; you are the branches. If a man remains in me and I in him, he will bear much fruit; apart from me you can do nothing. If anyone does not remain in me, he is like a branch that is thrown away and withers; such branches are picked up, thrown into the fire and burned. If you remain in me and my words remain in you, ask whatever you wish, and it will be given you. This is to my Father's glory, that you bear much fruit, showing yourselves to be my disciples."

Before Jesus sacrificed his life at Calvary, he gave his disciples this graphic allegory to communicate the necessity of remaining rooted in his teachings and life. He wanted his disciples to know that their relationship with him was vital, just as branches are to a vine. The culture of the vine was a common occupation in Palestine, and vineyards were everywhere. The vine was also the emblem of Israel, as symbolized by the great gold vine that adorned Herod's temple. But Jesus used the vine differently, applying it to one's spiritual life. When Jesus said that he is the True Vine, he was saying that apart from him we will spiritually die. Crucial to a vineyard is having the right stock, one that produces its own kind. In Jesus Christ we have heavenly stock that produces spiritual branches.

Israel was a noble vine and of the right seed, but they degenerated into a foreign species. The prophet Jeremiah wrote, "I planted you like a choice vine of sound and reliable stock. How then did you turn against me into a corrupt, wild vine?" In Jesus, we are a choice vine, but we can only bear fruit by being grafted into his life-sustaining roots. In nature, the vine is the nourishment that gives life to the branches. In like manner, Jesus nourishes those who remain united to him.

Jesus mentioned that his Father has the function of a gardener. As you know, a gardener nurtures and prunes the branches, so they might remain healthy and be productive. But a gardener also removes unproductive branches that are diseased and endanger the other branches. This is a clear message to individuals and churches whose relationship with God is an illusion. They may appear connected to Christ, but the disease of sin is killing what life may remain. Their lack of spiritual life shows their disconnection from the True Vine. But God prunes the faithful who bear fruit, making them even more productive. We can all testify that the process, although painful, is life-changing and glorious.

Jesus teaches that when we bear fruit we show ourselves to be his disciples, thereby glorifying the Father. If a tree is healthy it bears good fruit, and this pleases the owner, who has invested time and energy to make it possible. Our lives, and the fruit that we produce, will either draw people to Jesus or lead them away. As branches of the True Vine, what does our life reflect? Is the life of Jesus flowing through our veins? The apostle Paul said, "I live, yet not I, but Christ lives in me." Can we truly make this profession?

A LOVE STORY

Ruth 1:16–18

> Ruth said to Naomi, "Don't urge me to leave you or to turn back from you. Where you go I will go, and where you stay I will stay. Your people will be my people and your God my God. Where you die I will die, and there I will be buried. May the Lord deal with me, be it ever so severely, if anything but death separates you and me." When Naomi realized that Ruth was determined to go with her, she stopped urging her.

Ruth is the central figure in the book that is named after her. She is one of the most revered women in the Bible because of her abiding love for her mother-in-law Naomi, who was a Hebrew from Bethlehem. Naomi, her husband, and two sons, settled in Moab because of a famine in Judea. While in Moab her two sons married, and it was Mahlon who married a Moab woman named Ruth. However, tragedy struck the family, for not only did Naomi's husband die, but also her two sons. After this occurred, Naomi longed to return to the land of her birth, and after a period of time she and her daughter-in-law Ruth made the journey. The story ends with Ruth's marriage to Boaz and the birth of their son Obed.

In the brief four chapters of Ruth, her alien background is repeatedly stressed. People referred to her as Ruth the Moabites, the woman of Moab, or simply the stranger. But in spite of Israel's hatred of the Moabites, Ruth won the hearts of the Jewish people. In Bethlehem, she was admired for her love and commitment to her mother-in-law. Although the Bible provides no physical description of Ruth, literature and art have made every effort to reveal a woman with a pure spirit. Real beauty cannot be captured in a portrait or beheld with natural eyes, for it lies within a person. Its essence is truth and love, and this was Ruth's nature. She was everything that a godly person should be. She made a promise to Naomi, and she kept it. Rather than think only of herself, she chose to go to a country where she would be viewed as inferior and looked upon with suspicion. Even though Naomi tried to persuade Ruth not to leave her country, Ruth remained committed. She was willing to risk everything because of her love for her mother-in-law, knowing how Naomi suffered over the loss of her husband and two sons. Ruth wanted to be there for Naomi's needs. Although a young woman with her life ahead of her, she only saw her mother-in-law's pain.

The trip to Palestine was about 120 miles, and it was a dangerous journey for two women traveling alone. When they reached Bethlehem, Ruth did what she could to support the two of them. She worked menial jobs, even following reapers through the fields, gathering the grain left behind. One particular day she came into the field of Boaz, who was a wealthy landowner. He was also a distant relative of Naomi's deceased husband. More importantly, he was a man who was devoted to God. What more could a woman want? Boaz was immediately attracted to Ruth, and it was not long before there was a mutual love and marriage. From Boaz and Ruth came a son they named Obed who, with his parents, are in the genealogy of Jesus Christ.

Ruth could never have realized how the tragedies in her life would turn to blessings. Who could imagine that personal loss, poverty, and traveling to a foreign country, was God's plan. Ruth was rewarded for her love, faith, and commitment, at a time when everything seemed hopeless. Boaz revealed a powerful truth when he said to Ruth, "May you be richly rewarded by the

Lord, the God of Israel, under whose wings you have come to take refuge." May the truth of these words speak to our hearts and lives.

THE HARVEST

Mark 4:26–29

> This is what the kingdom of God is like. A man scatters seed on the ground. Night and day, whether he sleeps or gets up, the seed sprouts and grows, though he does not know how. All by itself the soil produces grain—first the stalk, then the head, then the full kernel in the head. As soon as the grain is ripe, he puts the sickle to it, because the harvest has come.

In this graphic analogy from nature, Jesus tells us that the building of God's kingdom is a mystery. Just as scattered seed goes through developmental stages on its own, so it is with the planting of the gospel. Both with nature and God's kingdom, there is a mysterious life force that takes the seed through the process that leads to fruition. With seeds of the gospel, the mystery speaks to the work of the Holy Spirit, who prepares the heart to receive the seed. While some hearts can be compared to hard soil, not allowing the seed to penetrate, the wind will eventually carry the seed to a place where it will take root.

In a spiritual sense, the Church has been planted by God with the expectation of a harvest. There will come a time when the Lord, satisfied with the harvest, will put forth his sickle. When this occurs, only the ripened grain will be harvested. After all, what good is seed that remains dormant and fails to develop. In nature, the stalk coming up through the ground is the first stage of life, but we know that some stalks never blossom. In their dying state, they are destroyed by insects, fowl, and the weather. Many people encounter this plight with their spiritual lives. They may initially show signs of spiritual conversion, but it is short-lived by the unwillingness to grow. As seen in the parable of the *Four Soils*, seed does not always fall upon fertile ground. It is only the fertile heart, being those totally committed in faith, who will bear fruit and be brought into God's kingdom. The Lord's sickle will not destroy the ripened grain, for it will separate the full kernel from the unproductive seed and dead growth. You might say that the action of the sickle is the parting stroke or final act.

Everyone is summoned to examine their spiritual development, to determine their present stage of growth. Are we ready for the Great Harvest? God created us out of love, and he commands that we become servants of that love. This necessitates that we continuously pray for the mind, attitude, and heart that brings glory to our Creator. It is not enough that we profess Christianity or align ourselves with a particular church group. We are called to begin the sanctifying process that brings us into an intimate relationship with Jesus Christ. The apostle Paul told believers that they were to move beyond the milk stage to that of solid food. He urged them to grow in the teachings and love of Christ, taking on the divine nature of the Savior.

It is difficult to understand why people are content to remain at the starting gate, refusing to exercise their faith. The Church is reflective of those societal attitudes that seek the easiest path in life. Rather than exercising the discipline that brings spiritual strength and maturity, there is a tendency to merely affiliate oneself with Christ and the Church. Let us not forget that discipleship is not simply church membership, but rather a life that is rooted in the Lord.

Eleven

SERVANTHOOD

LIFE'S TWO PATHS

Psalm 36:1–4, 12, 13

> An oracle is within my heart concerning the sinfulness of the wicked. There is no fear of God before his eyes. For in his own eyes he flatters himself too much to detect or hate his sin. The words of his mouth are wicked and deceitful; he has ceased to be wise and to do good. Even on his bed he plots evil; he commits himself to a sinful course and does not reject what is wrong. The wicked plot against the righteous and gnash their teeth at them; but the Lord laughs at the wicked, for he knows their day is coming.

These words, which were written by King David, reveal his thoughts concerning the wicked. He tells us that their self-concept is one of pride and arrogance, and their thoughts and deeds are destructive. They always seek to flatter themselves at the expense of others, giving no thought to their own sinfulness. Instead of following the humble path of the Lord, they see themselves as being special. Like the self-righteous Pharisees of the New Testament, the wicked see only their own desires and needs. They believe that they have total control over their lives.

If your eyes are only on yourself, it is impossible to see God and the concerns of other people. In fact, there is no need for the Lord, and our relationship with others is self-serving. The apostle James gives warning to the proud, telling them that they will surely fall. To the Christians in Rome, Paul wrote,

"Do not think of yourselves more highly than you ought. But rather think of yourself with sober judgment." He also said, "May I never boast except in the cross of our Lord Jesus Christ, through which the world has been crucified to me, and I to the world. Neither circumcision or uncircumcision means anything; what matters is a new creation." Paul teaches that we should have the same attitude as Jesus Christ, who humbled himself and became obedient to God, even to the point of death by crucifixion.

The path to the Father and all blessings is through the intercession of Jesus. Of the Jews, our Savior said, "Look, your house is left to you desolate. I tell you, you will not see me again until you say, 'Blessed is he who comes in the name of the Lord.'" This is also the message for the Church, for until we come to Jesus in faith and humility, we will not see salvation. Like the congregation in Ephesus, many individuals and churches have forsaken their first love, who is Jesus Christ. They have replaced Christ with worldliness and have twisted biblical truths to satisfy their sinful lifestyles. Human will, pride, and self-righteousness, have replaced the path of holiness. May we never forget that everything we have is a gift, and without God's mercy we would be lost.

Although some people look for a middle road, there are only two paths in life. One leads to eternal peace and joy in God's kingdom, while the other is the road to outer darkness. These are two distinct lives, for we either follow Christ and plant seeds of love and forgiveness, or we sow bitterness and hatred. The choice has always been a matter of the will. As we examine our life's journey, are we truly on the path of divine love? Do we ever try to walk down two roads at the same time? Although the road to God is less traveled, it is the only one that brings fulfillment and happiness.

MAKING A DECISION

Matthew 27:11–17, 21, 22

> Jesus stood before the governor, and the governor asked him, "Are you the king of the Jews?" "Yes, it is as you say," Jesus replied. When he was accused by the chief priests and the elders, he gave no answer. Then Pilate asked him, "Don't you hear how many things they are accusing you of?" But Jesus made no reply, not even to a single charge—to the great amazement of the governor. Now it was the governor's custom at the feast to release a prisoner chosen by the crowd. At that time they had a notorious prisoner called Barabbas. So when the crowd had gathered, Pilate asked them, "Which one do you want me to release to you: Barabbas, or Jesus, who is called Christ?" "Barabbas," they answered.

"What shall I do, then, with Jesus who is called Christ?" Pilate asked. They all answered, "Crucify him!"

What you have read was a democratic election that took place almost two thousand years ago. It occurred in a country that was not a democracy, but rather one that was under Roman rule and occupation. Without question, it was the most significant election known to humanity, with the outcome being influenced by Israel's religious elite. This was not an election that was full of political pomp or promises. There were no platform platitudes, catchy phrases, buttons, or balloons.

The election was democratic because the people could choose between two individuals, and their vote was clear. They chose Jesus to be executed and Barabbas to be set free. Each Passover, it was customary for the Roman government to set one prisoner free. It was the governor's way of keeping peace with the people, who could get aggressive during the Passover season. Pilate knew that Jesus was innocent, but he allowed the people to make the decision. For Jesus to be crucified under Roman law, the charge of treason was necessary. If Jesus claimed to be a king, when the sole ruler was Caesar, it was a crime punishable by death. The original charge brought by the religious leaders was blasphemy, which was only a violation under Jewish religious laws.

This was an execution that had prophetic overtones, for the crucifixion of one man set another one free. In reality, it is the death of Jesus that sets all of us free from the penalty of sin. Barabbas was a condemned man without hope, and then out of nowhere came Jesus, who would give him life. We see ourselves in this election, for we also are condemned sinners without hope. But Jesus Christ came to free us through his sacrificial death. There was a celebration when Barabbas was released, and such is the case with us. The heavens celebrate the life of every sinner who has been pardoned through the death of Christ.

What is interesting about this election is that Pontius Pilate took part in it. Even though he claimed to have washed his hands of the matter, he cast a vote by allowing an innocent man to be crucified. But we also exercise our free will and choice concerning Jesus. Every day we cast a ballot by the choices we make and the life that we live. As Jesus stood before Pilate and the Jews, he continuously stands before us with his words of truth and conviction. To decide for Christ is to cast your life at his feet, and be willing to carry the cross of sacrifice. It is assuming his nature and living the life of a humble servant.

THE COST OF DISCIPLESHIP
Luke 9:57–62

> As they were walking along the road, a man said to him, "I will follow you wherever you go." Jesus replied, "Foxes have holes and the birds of the air have nests, but the Son of Man has nowhere to lay his head." He said to another man, "Follow me." But the man replied, "Lord, first let me go and bury my father." Jesus said to him, "Let the dead bury their own dead, but you go and proclaim the kingdom of God." Still another said, "I will follow you, Lord; but first let me go back and say good-by to my family." Jesus replied, "No one who puts his hand to the plow and looks back is fit for service in the kingdom of God."

In this discourse Jesus addresses the cost of discipleship, and the excuses that people use not to follow him. While our Savior and his disciples were walking to Jerusalem, Luke reports that he spoke to three men along the way. The first man told Jesus that he would follow him anywhere, but Jesus was quick to point out the cost involved. Our Lord wanted him to know that it was not an easy life, for a person will never know what will be required of them. It is apparent that this man changed his mind, for he did not respond to Jesus. The second man was actually called by Jesus, but he wanted to first bury his father. Who could deny such a request? But the request was to stay home until his father died, and this meant an indefinite delay. Jesus told him that the work of the kingdom could not be delayed. The third man offered his services, with the stipulation that he first say good-by to his family. Although this doesn't sound unreasonable, Jesus searched his heart and knew that it was just a delay. Our Lord then said, "No one who puts his hand to the plow and looks back is fit for service in God's kingdom." This simply means that you cannot follow Christ and yearn for the life that you left behind.

When Jesus says, "Follow me," it is a call from the old life. The three men that Jesus spoke to could not break away from the life they were living. To step out and trust Jesus was too difficult for them, and they responded with excuses. Taking up the cross and following Jesus means self-sacrifice and obedience, a life that few people are willing to pursue. In all decisions there is a cost to be considered, and discipleship is no different. Jesus said, "I do not seek my own will, but the will of him who sent me." When we seek God's will for our lives, we may be taken down a path that we do not desire to travel. The joy, however, is knowing that we are serving and sharing in our Lord's work. When we follow Jesus we discover the true meaning in life, and we reach spiritual heights never imagined.

An excuse not to follow our Savior is not a pardon, but rather an answer. The Lord has heard every conceivable excuse, but the one who searches the heart cannot be deceived. When the three men in our story thought about leaving the comfort and security of their present life, they made a decision not to follow Jesus. These men were offered life, and they chose to walk in darkness. They were given the opportunity to experience God's glory, and they chose to remain where they were. So many people settle for what the world offers, rather than the gifts of God. We are called to put the past behind us, that we might realize our potential in Christ.

BEING A SERVANT

Matthew 20:20–28

> Then the mother of Zebedee's sons came to Jesus with her sons and, kneeling down, asked a favor of him. "What is it you want?" he asked. She said, "Grant that one of these two sons of mine may sit at your right and the other at your left in your kingdom." "You don't know what you are asking," Jesus said to them. "Can you drink the cup I am going to drink?" "We can," they answered. Jesus said to them, "You will indeed drink from my cup, but to sit at my right or left is not for me to grant. These places belong to those for whom they have been prepared by my Father." When the ten heard about this, they were indignant with the two brothers. Jesus called them together and said, "You know that the rulers of the Gentiles lord it over them, and their high officials exercise authority over them. Not so with you. Instead, whoever wants to become great among you must be your servant, and whoever wants to be first must be your slave—just as the Son of Man did not come to be served, but to give his life as a ransom for many."

Jesus informed his disciples that greatness is found in being a servant to others. He continued by saying that whoever wants to be first must be a slave. These were strange and shocking words coming from someone considered to be a Jewish teacher in the first century. Actually, this is a radical teaching today, even amongst some Christians. How can greatness be found in being a servant or slave to others? If the word *servant* wasn't puzzling enough, his reference to being a *slave* certainly was.

Jesus came to us as a humble servant, giving his life for all who receive him in faith. There was nothing in his life and ministry that was self-serving. His suffering and death was the Father's salvation plan, with Jesus willfully giving his life for the sins of the world. If our Master lived his life as a servant, how can we do otherwise? In fact, Jesus calls us to take up his cross and to walk in his footsteps. Sharing in the life and ministry of Christ requires that we place ourselves in another person's position. It means seeing others as being better than us, a reality that is only possible through persistent prayer and a surrendered life. Only when we prayerfully surrender to the teachings of our Savior can we possess his humility.

It is the servant's life that has true meaning and purpose. When we move beyond ourselves and touch the lives of others we experience an inner transformation. Rather than a life that excludes or judges other people, we begin to feel their heartache and pain. It is at this point that we have passed from death to life. One can only imagine what the Church and world would be like if everyone possessed the heart of a servant. Unlike the world's understanding of life and relationships, it is the servant who is great in God's eyes. Those who treat everyone with respect, trying to feel their anguish and suffering, are the true disciples. When we look for the good in all people, reaching out to them with concrete acts of love, we are sharing in the mission of Christ.

Jesus set aside his heavenly glory to become a servant to humanity. He, who is one with the Father and Holy Spirit, became a servant to save us from sin and death. If you are searching for greatness, a life that will impact upon the lives of others, then you must look to the sacrificial life of Christ as your example. Jesus told his followers that those who live only for themselves will lose their life. They will forfeit eternal life in God's glorious kingdom. To have life, both now and forever, requires that you have a servant's heart. Is this your desire and prayer?

KNOWING GOD'S WILL

Romans 12:1, 2

> Therefore, I urge you, brothers, in view of God's mercy, to offer your bodies as living sacrifices, holy and pleasing to God—which is your spiritual worship. Do not conform any longer to the pattern of this world, but be transformed by the renewing of your mind. Then you will be able to test and approve what God's will is—his good, pleasing and perfect will.

In this letter Paul is making an appeal to the Christians in Rome, that they present their entire lives as living sacrifices to God. He says that by doing so they will know what the Lord's will is for them. The Jews presented God with animal sacrifices to symbolize the offering up of themselves in holy living, but they missed the point. Rather than realizing the spiritual significance of their offerings, the sacrifices became a source of pride. Because of sin, they failed to see the graphic picture that God had painted for them.

Paul told the people that the Lord wants living sacrifices. He said that only through personal surrender will we know God's perfect will. We have one life, and it is this life that we are to offer up to the Lord. Regardless of where we are in our journey, God wants us to give our all to him. When the Israelites sacrificed animals, every part was surrendered to the Lord. The entire animal was consumed, with no part being wasted. This is the message God intended for his people, but it was lost to pride.

As living sacrifices, we become aware of God's personal plan for our lives. Rather than searching for God's will, it naturally unfolds through our surrender. This is realized when we reflect upon our past. We find that even insignificant events played a part in how God was molding and using us as his vessels. There is also the inner peace and fulfillment that accompanies our submission to God's plan. We were created to serve God and one another in the spirit of love, and only when we walk in this light can we truly receive the grace that makes us whole. The word *sacrifice* denotes completion, meaning that our lives are to be a complete surrender. If you recall, both Cain and Abel offered up sacrifices to the Lord, but God did not look with favor upon Cain's offering. Although we are not told why, we can assume that Cain's heart was not in his offering. A true and complete sacrifice involves a pure heart.

Over the years, I have heard how people struggle in their search for the Lord's will. Many of these individuals were looking for a clear event that would signal a direction for them, and when it did not occur they lost the incentive to pray. People have difficulty believing that God's will is an unfolding process. Through our continuous surrender, the Lord directs us to opportunities for service. God's will involves every aspect of our lives, not simply one's profession or Church-related activities. Paul said, "I urge you, in view of God's mercy, to offer your bodies as living sacrifices, holy and pleasing to God. Then you will be able to test and approve what God's will is."

A MOTHER'S PROMISE

I Samuel 1:10–13

> Hannah wept much and prayed to the Lord. And she made a vow, saying, "O Lord Almighty, if you will only look upon your servant's misery and remember me, and not forget your servant, but give her a son, then I will give him to the Lord for all the days of his life, and no razor will ever be used on

his head." As she kept on praying to the Lord, Eli observed her mouth. Hannah was praying in her heart and her lips were moving, but her voice was not heard.

This is a story about a promise that was made, and one that was kept. Hannah was the mother of Samuel, but for many years she was unable to conceive. She relentlessly prayed to the Lord for a son, whom she could love and dedicate to God's service. Hannah valued motherhood, knowing that children are a gift from the Creator to bring fulfillment to one's life. For a long time it seemed that having a child was not God's will for her, but she never stopped praying. She told God that if he blessed her with a son, she would take him to Eli, who would mentor him in priestly duties.

The Lord searched Hannah's heart and knew that she was a faithful servant who always sought to walk a righteous path. God was pleased with her life, as well as her intentions regarding the birth of a child. Her motives before the Lord were pure, and the Lord responded to her request. Hannah was blessed with a son whom she named Samuel, which means *a request from God*. She dedicated Samuel as a Nazarite, taking him to Shiloh. It was there that he served under Eli and experienced revelations from the Lord.

Samuel became recognized as a judge, who eventually ruled the entire government. It was Samuel who appointed Saul as king of Israel, and who later reproved Saul and anointed David to replace him. Samuel's life revealed the faith and obedience of his mother Hannah, who was his earliest influence and example in life. He became one of the Lord's greatest servants, whose advice to Israel was the motto of his life. He told the people to serve the Lord with all their heart.

Hannah recognized her responsibilities before the Lord, that of being a committed mother and model of holiness for her son. She also remembered her promise to God, and she did everything possible to keep that promise. Her pledge to the Lord changed an entire nation and the course of Israel's history. We must never underestimate the impact of a life that is offered up to God. Throughout history we find holy people who have made a difference in the world. We have all experienced people whose love and faith made a difference in our lives. There have been many individuals in my life who have served as examples and mentors, but the greatest was my mother. It was through her prayers and quiet witness that I accepted Jesus Christ into my life.

Parents have no guarantee that their children will follow the Lord, but what chance do our children have without a spiritual foundation and example? Parents are given the responsibility to teach their children the way of the Lord, and this is done through prayer, instruction, discipline, and example. As we examine our lives, have we truly kept our promise to raise our children in the Church?

A LESSON ON GIVING

Mark 12:41–44

> Jesus sat down opposite the place where the offerings were put and watched the crowd putting their money into the temple treasury. Many rich people threw in large amounts. But a poor widow came and put in two very small copper coins, worth only a fraction of a penny. Calling his disciples to him, Jesus said, "I tell you the truth, this poor widow has put more into the treasury than all the others. They all gave out of their wealth; but she out of poverty put in everything—all that she had to live on."

Jesus used the sacrificial giving of a poor widow to teach his disciples a valuable lesson. The temple treasury was a chest, which had a trumpet-shaped spout to receive the coins. The money that was received was devoted to the service of the temple. Mark tells us that Jesus sat down opposite the treasury and observed the people and the amount of money that they were giving. We learn that some of the wealthy folks gave large sums of money, but the Lord's focus was not upon them. Instead, it was on a poor widow, who under normal circumstances would have gone unnoticed. If she only knew that the Son of God was observing her. Jesus, being aware of her situation, knew that she gave all that she possessed. In fact, unlike those who gave out of their surplus, she gave out of her poverty. Sometimes we forget that God measures our giving by what we keep, rather than the amount given.

The coins that the widow gave were the smallest in use amongst the Jews. While the precise amount cannot be estimated today, it was probably a fraction of our penny. Now, if we were to put this amount into a collection plate, I am certain that our story would also be told, but not in the same manner. The widow's giving revealed more love, faith, and self-denial, than the larger offerings of those with more means. When we sacrificially give to the Lord's work, we are living our faith, trusting in God to meet our needs. We are also establishing priorities in our life.

The Church treasury is of supreme importance for spreading the gospel message and reaching out to people in need. It was necessary during the ministry of Jesus, when people contributed to the needs of the disciples and the poor, and it is required today. All missions in life depend upon financial support, and the Church is no different. The treasury of any congregation is a measure of the people's faith and love, as well as their excitement for the work that is being done in Jesus' name. God wants people who cheerfully give from their hearts, rather than from a sense of obligation or duty. Everything we have is a gift from the Lord, and he requires that we give a small portion back that others might also be blessed. The 10 percent principle is not a pathway to heaven, but it is a guide to help us. If we did not have this principle, some people would try to buy their way into heaven, while others would give nothing.

The greatness of a gift is measured by its effectiveness, and we know that God multiplies every gift. The widow's gift was small by our standards, but look at the effects. She not only gave to the temple in Jerusalem, but she has also given to millions of people over the generations who have read this story. Jesus has used her small, but sacrificial gift, to touch our hearts and renew our spirits. We now know what it means to both give and receive God's blessings.

AN ETERNAL INVESTMENT

Matthew 25:14–22, 24–26, 28–30

> The kingdom of God will be like a man going on a journey, who called his servants and entrusted his property to them. To one he gave five talents of money, to another two talents, and to another one talent, each according to his ability. Then he went on his journey. The man who had received the five talents went at once and put his money to work and gained five more. So also, the one with the two talents gained two more. But the man who had received the one talent went off, dug a hole in the ground and hid his master's money. After a long time the master of those servants returned and settled accounts with them. The man who had received the five talents brought the other five. "Master," he said, "you entrusted me with five talents. See, I have gained five more." His master replied, "Well done, good and faithful servant! You have been faithful with a few things. I will put you in charge of many things. Come, and share your master's happiness!" The man with the two talents also came. "Master," he said, "you entrusted me with two talents; see I have gained two more." Then the man who had received the one talent came. "Master," he said, "I knew that you are a hard man, harvesting where you have not sown and gathered where you have not scattered seed. So I was afraid and went out and hid your talent in the ground. See, here is what belongs to you." His master replied, "You wicked, lazy servant! So you knew that I harvest where I have not sown and gather where I have not scattered seed. Take the talent from him, and give it to the one who has ten talents. For everyone who has will be given more, and he will have an abundance. Whoever does not have, even what he has will be taken from him.

And throw that worthless servant outside, into the darkness, where there will be weeping and gnashing of teeth."

This is a story about investments, which is a subject that everyone can identify with, including people during the time of Christ. Regardless of where we are in life, we are all investment-minded. When we hear the word *investment*, we tend to think about financial matters, such as the stock market or retirement accounts. When and how we use our finances affects every aspect of our life. Recently, I was having dental work done and had to make a decision. Was I going to invest in crowns, which the dentist had suggested? After thinking about my age, as well as my limited income as a retired pastor, I concluded that it was not a good investment. After all, it is only a matter of time when more teeth will need to be crowned. Why spend thousands of dollars when the end result will be custom-made teeth that I can take in and out. Whether it is a medical decision, the purchase of an expensive item such as a car or home, or simply taking a vacation, we want to make good investments. Even when we purchase candy bars, we want the most sugar for our money. So, what is the point to all of this?

In our text Jesus is talking about investments. In this simple and graphic lesson, he is addressing a timeless subject. How we invest, not only speaks to the present, but also to our future. In this case, Jesus is referring to our eternal future. As we consider this teaching, we are confronted with our inner life and how it impacts upon us. Actually, we are forced to look at investments in a way that few people think about. What are we doing with the gifts that the Lord has bestowed upon us? Are we using our God-given talents for a higher purpose?

The story Jesus told reveals three men, all of whom were given gifts to invest for their master. Although each man was given a different amount to invest, the master's intention was the same for all three. They were to take what was given to them and invest it during the master's absence. As you read, two of the men were obedient, but the third individual was not. Instead of investing his talent, he was full of lame excuses.

There is a timeless truth here, for the centuries have not changed human nature. The master took the talent away from the disobedient servant and gave it to the one whose investment made the most profit. This is what happens to the disobedient that refuse to invest what God has given to them. What they received will be taken away and given to those who will use their gifts to serve the Lord.

God gives each of us gifts, along with the opportunities to multiply them through a surrendered life. But in the Master's absence, are we investing the gifts that have been entrusted to us? Do our lives reflect the love of Christ in all that we think, say, and do? When the Master returns what will he find when he calls us to account? Will it be spiritual laziness and disobedience, or will Jesus invite us to share in his joy? Unlike the wicked servant, we must never hide our gifts from a world that desperately needs them. Through the investment of our lives, the Lord is able to reach the world for whom Jesus gave his life.

MARY FOUND FAVOR WITH GOD

Luke 1:26–35, 38

> In the sixth month, God sent the angel Gabriel to Nazareth, a town in Galilee, to a virgin pledged to be married to a man named Joseph, a descendant of David. The virgin's name was Mary. The angel went to her and said, "Greetings, you who are highly favored! The Lord is with you." Mary was greatly troubled at his words and wondered what kind of greeting this might be. But the angel said to her, "Do not be afraid, Mary, you have found favor with God. You will be with child and give birth to a son, and you are to give him the name Jesus. He will be great and will be called the Son of the Most High. The Lord God will give him the throne of his Father David, and he will reign over the house of Jacob forever; his kingdom will never end." "How will this be," Mary asked the angel, "since I am a virgin?" The angel answered, "The Holy Spirit will come upon you, and the power of the Most High will overshadow you. So the holy one to be born will be called the Son of God." "I am the Lord's servant," Mary answered. "May it be to me as you have said." Then the angel left her.

The message that the archangel Gabriel gave to Mary would change both her life and the world. In a shocking announcement, Gabriel told Mary that she was God's chosen vessel who would bring his Son into the world. When Mary heard this she was frightened and confused. What did this mean, and why did she find favor with the Lord? Certainly there were many women in Palestine whom God could have chosen. In terms of the world, Mary had no special significance. In fact, all indications reveal that she was from a poor family. This is substantiated by the pigeon offerings that she made to the Lord. Those of small means could not afford the larger animals.

In her bewilderment, Mary was concerned about how others would respond to this announcement. In addition to her family and friends, how would Joseph receive this news? They were soon to be married, and this raised some difficult issues. But regardless of the confusion, anxiety, and fear, Mary was full of praise and thanksgiving. She knew that the Lord was about to touch her life in a way never imagined, that somehow God would use her for his glory. Mary had no idea what the future held, but she was certain that her life would be in God's hands and follow a plan according to his will. Without more answers and understanding, she surrendered her life to God, saying, "I am the Lord's servant, may it be to me as you have said." What a moving insight into this humble woman, one that speaks to us in a powerful way. When we are uncertain about the path our life is taking, are we able to echo Mary's words of surrender and trust?

When Mary visited her cousin Elizabeth, who would soon be the mother of John the Baptist, both women were filled with joy. Elizabeth said to Mary, "Why am I so favored, that the mother of my Lord should come to me. Blessed are you among women, and blessed is the child you will bear." Mary then said, "My soul praises the Lord, and my spirit rejoices in God my Savior, for he has been mindful of the humble state of his servant. From now on all generations will call me blessed, for the Mighty One has done great things for me—holy is his name."

Mary had no idea that she was about to embark upon a journey of heartache that would lead to Calvary. Sometimes we forget that finding favor with the Lord does not mean a life without sacrifice and pain. But Mary never took her eyes off of God, knowing that her suffering was for a higher purpose. Although she could not comprehend the events that would take place, her surrender to the Lord was total. The life that was laid out for Mary was filled with trials, but she never wavered in her trust and commitment.

The Lord knew that Mary had a pure heart and the faith of a child. Regardless of her young age and the road of sorrows that she would travel, she was willing to sacrifice everything for God's glory. Even at the crucifixion, while watching the agonizing death of Jesus, she remained faithful to God. She made a promise, and she kept that promise to the very end. Through her surrender, Mary brought the seed of forgiveness and salvation into the world.

We will never know the complete path that is set before us or the sacrifices and pain along the way, but we can be assured that our calling will bless the lives of other people. What matters is that we trust in the perfect wisdom of our Creator and prayerfully walk in his will, knowing that we are his vessels of grace. The Lord promised Mary a child who would be conceived in a mysterious way. Her son was to be called *Savior* and the *Son of the Most High*. Although Mary saw the glory of Jesus' resurrection, it was only after a long and painful journey. While life can be a struggle that is filled with sorrow, fulfillment and purpose is realized when we commit our lives to God. The Lord places his trust in us, to be his instruments of healing and reconciliation. This does not mean a trouble-free life, but we are blessed when our obedience bears fruit for ourselves and others.

DAVID'S CALL

I Samuel 16:1, 10–13

> The Lord said to Samuel, "How long will you mourn for Saul, since I have rejected him as king over Israel? Fill your horn with oil, and be on your way; I am sending you to Jesse of Bethlehem. I have chosen one of his sons to be king." Jesse had seven of his sons pass before Samuel, but Samuel said to him, "The Lord has not chosen these." So he asked Jesse, "Are these all the sons you have?" "There is still the youngest," Jesse answered, "but he is tending the sheep." Samuel said, "Send for him; we will not sit down until he arrives." So he went and had him brought in. He was ruddy, with a fine appearance and handsome features. The Lord said, "Rise and anoint him; he is the one." So Samuel took the horn of oil and anointed him in the presence of his brothers, and from that day on the Spirit of the Lord came upon David in power.

King Saul was an impressive man, with the outer appearance of what one would look for in a leader. He was tall and handsome, standing head and shoulders over the people. At the mere sight of him the nation cheered, for he was a mighty force against Israel's enemies. One by one his army struck down the Philistines, Ammonites, Moabites, Amalekites, and Syrians. But at the height of his popularity everything fell apart. Drunk with power, he ignored God's voice. His articulate mind began to crumble, with the result being fits of madness, jealousy, and melancholy. Then, after losing a battle and being mortally wounded, he intentionally fell upon his own sword. The Philistines hacked off his head, and they hung his body on their city wall.

It was prior to Saul's death that God decided to replace him as Israel's king, and the Lord called Samuel to anoint a new leader. The past was not to be pondered, for it was time for a new beginning. Samuel was no longer to grieve over Saul's situation. He was now given the task of anointing one of Jesse's sons to be Saul's successor. Jesse had seven sons pass before Samuel, some of whom had strong physical appearances, such as Eliab. But the Lord made it known that none of these men were to be anointed. Little did Samuel know that the next king of Israel would be Jesse's youngest son David, who was out tending the sheep. When David appeared before Samuel, the Lord immediately said, "Rise and anoint him. He is the one." Upon his anointing, the power of the Holy Spirit came upon David.

What does all this say to us? Actually, it is a story of encouragement, for regardless of our age or status, we can be used for God's glory. Like Mary the mother of Jesus, David was very young when God chose him to be an instrument of divine grace. It is interesting how God takes individuals who are ignored by the world, and uses them in a powerful way. Unlike the world, the Lord does not look at the outer person. Instead, he looks for a pure and willing spirit. These are the individuals who will remain faithful and committed to God's work.

Saul's self-serving disobedience is a lesson for everyone. He was a man who had it all, until he decided to go his own way. The one who started out listening for God's voice, became a victim of power and the people's praises. A once great king, he lost sight of his calling. But this is the picture of many people, who obey God until pride and self-desires consume them. Jesus refers to these individuals as being lukewarm, and he places them in the context of the lost. As we examine our hearts, are we willing to continuously listen to the Lord's voice and follow his will?

THE HEALING WATERS

II Kings 2:19–22

> The men of the city said to Elisha, "Look, our lord, this town is well situated as you can see, but the water is bad, and the land is unproductive." "Bring me a new bowl," he said, "and put salt in it." So they brought it to him. Then he went out to the spring, and threw salt into it, saying, "This is what the Lord says: 'I have healed this water. Never again will it cause death or make the land unproductive.'" And the water has remained wholesome to this day, according to the word Elisha had spoken.

After the prophet Elijah was taken up to heaven in a whirlwind and chariot of fire, Elisha took the mantle that fell from him. He took it to the Jordan River, where he struck the waters with it, asking, "Where is the Lord, the God of Elijah?" As he struck the waters, they immediately divided. This was the Lord's seal upon Elisha that he truly was Elijah's successor. All that was now needed were words and acts that would convince the people that he was God's chosen prophet.

Elisha's first task as a prophet involved the purification of water. Knowing that he was a man of God, the men of Jericho approached him, asking if he would do something about their water pollution. Jericho had come under a curse, and all their wealth and knowledge could not cleanse the water. What a frustrating situation when the intellect and money cannot change things. Although Jericho was a beautiful city on the outside, with great potential, the people could not survive with the poor condition of the water. Like people who have a pleasant exterior and great potential, inner pollution destroys their life. We also learn that the ground of the city was barren and thus unfruitful. Labor as they may, the people were unable to obtain results. Such is the state of those who are polluted within, making it impossible for the fruit of the Spirit to develop and grow.

The cure for the contaminated water is both interesting and profound. Elisha asked for a new bowl, which he filled with salt. He then emptied the salt into the water, declaring that it was purified. When Elisha emptied the salt into the water the people could identify with the symbolism, because salt is a purifier that destroys bacteria and fights infection. The salt, of course, was symbolic of God's purifying and healing power. Elisha asked for a new bowl, indicating that through the Lord all things become new. This is a fitting emblem for the New Covenant through Jesus Christ, who is the salt of our salvation, offering spiritual healing and a new life.

Elisha cast the salt into the spring at the source of the water flow, rather than in the open stream. By doing this he went straight to the cause of the pollution. This allowed the salt to make its way from the spring into the open waters. With us, the salt is Jesus Christ, and the source is our heart. Only when Jesus is in our heart will life's pathway be cleansed. God sent Elisha to heal the waters of Jericho, and he sent his Son to heal the human heart. Jesus said to the woman at the well, "If you knew who I am, you would ask me for living water, and you would thirst no more." As we walk in the Spirit, we continuously receive the pure and living water offered by our Savior.

A HUMBLE LIFE

Philippians 2:1–8

> If you have any encouragement from being united with Christ, if any comfort from his love, if any fellowship with the Spirit, if any tenderness and compassion, then make my joy complete by being like-minded, having the same love, being one in spirit and purpose. Do nothing out of selfish ambition or vain conceit, but in humility consider others better than yourselves. Each of you should look not only to your own interests, but also to the interests of others. Your attitude should be the same as that of Christ Jesus: Who being in the very nature God, did not consider equality with God something to be grasped, but made himself nothing, taking the very nature of a servant, being made in

human likeness. And being found in appearance as a man, he humbled himself and became obedient to death—even death on a cross.

Paul reminded Christians that Jesus entered this world as a servant. The one, who with the Father and Holy Spirit is glorified, came to humanity as a vessel of mercy and grace. When Jesus came to earth he emptied himself of heaven's glory to live a life of self-sacrifice. In Christ we see a suffering servant who chose to experience both our joy and pain. He is a Savior who completely identifies with the human condition, experiencing all of our emotions and trials. But Jesus suffered more than physical and emotional pain. His separation from the Father at the time of death, along with his descent into hell, is an agony that is beyond our comprehension. In Jesus Christ we have a Savior who has forever bonded with the humanity that he created, who will eternally bear the scars of a love that has no limits or bounds. They are the wounds of a life that was willfully given for all sinners. Only as a suffering servant could Jesus fully know human anguish, pain, and death, and it is this suffering that has aroused his compassion and mercy for us.

There is nothing in our Savior's nature that is self-serving, for his total life has been given for our forgiveness and salvation. He came as one who was led like a lamb to the slaughter. His life reveals the very essence of God's love, providing us with the perfect example. As we take up the cross and follow Christ, we become one with the nature of God. Through precept and example, he calls us to the world's mission fields. Our witness of love begins within our personal environment, and it extends to every opportunity that God makes possible. Jesus said to his disciples, "The greatest among you will be your servant. For whoever exalts himself will be humbled, and whoever humbles himself will be exalted." Jesus assures us that whatever we do for the least of his children, we do it for him, meaning that we share in his compassion and mercy for all people. We can add to this truth by saying, whatever we do for others we also do for ourselves. It is through reaching out to others that God's grace flows into our lives.

Jesus teaches that we lose our lives when we try to save them. This implies that those who give of themselves will find eternal life. But we must give expecting nothing in return. We serve others because we are rooted in the love and teachings of Jesus. Living as a servant is only possible through the death of the old person. When the sinful part is crucified, a new life is resurrected.

Twelve

GIFTS OF THE SPIRIT

ONE IN SPIRIT

Philippians 2:1–7

> If you have any encouragement from being united with Christ, if any comfort from his love, if any fellowship with the Spirit, if any tenderness and compassion, then make my joy complete by being like-minded, having the same love, being one in spirit and purpose. Do nothing out of selfish ambition or vain conceit, but in humility consider others better than yourselves. Each of you should look not only to your own interests, but also to the interests of others. Your attitude should be the same as that of Christ Jesus, who being in very nature God, did not consider equality with God something to be grasped, but made himself nothing, taking the very nature of a servant, and being made in human likeness.

This text is about all relationships, with the emphasis being upon those within the Church. Paul's writings emphasize that Jesus is the thread that binds us together. For Paul, harmonious fellowship is an absolute if we are to call ourselves Christians. In fact, he states that the lack of interpersonal harmony is inconceivable and a contradiction to the teachings of Christ. Paul repeatedly calls for harmony and unity amongst believers, stressing that the Church is one body, with each member belonging to the other. His epistles tell us we are baptized by one Spirit and receive the same hope.

How much thought do we give to our relationships? Do we continuously pray about them and take initiatives toward reconciliation when needed? According to Paul, to be united with Christ is to be united with one another in love and purpose. The Church is a community that must reveal the one person of Jesus Christ. In the body of Christ there is no room for the sins of pride and self-will, nor is there room for complaining spirits. There is room, however, for more love, understanding, tolerance, and humility. Humility is central to our spiritual journey because it decreases self-power, thereby uniting us with God and one another. This tells us why there is no Godly relationship apart from humility.

The apostle Paul exhorts us to be like-minded and to be one in spirit. But we cannot communicate what we do not possess, and here lies the problem with so many people. Although they have biblical knowledge and an affiliation with the Church, they lack the love of Christ. The fellowship that is rooted in the humility of Jesus is absent. Paul told fellow believers that, when possible, they should be at peace with everyone. However, he stressed that Christians must pay special attention to their relationships. After all, if there is no love in the Church, then where can it be found? Also, how can we be communicators and witnesses of the gospel without love and unity? The world is searching for the love that is found in Jesus Christ, and we are to mirror that love. Without the love of Christ, the Church is simply a worldly institution that just happens to be tax-free.

In his prayer to the Father for all believers, Jesus said, "I have given them the glory that you gave me, that they may be one, as we are one. May they be brought to complete unity, to let the world know that you sent me and have loved them." Jesus said to his disciples, "My command to you is this, that you love one another, as I have loved you." Without the love of Christ, we are empty vessels that are unable to reveal God and be united in his Spirit.

THE CONTENT LIFE

Philippians 4:10–13

> I rejoice greatly in the Lord that at last you have renewed your concern for me. Indeed, you have been concerned, but you had no opportunity to show it. I am not saying this because I am in need, for I have learned to be content whatever the circumstances. I know what it is like to be in need, and I know what it is to have plenty. I have learned the secret of being content in any and every situation, whether well fed or hungry, whether living in plenty or in want. I can do everything through him who gives me strength.

In this letter Paul is thanking the Galatians for their concerns and gifts, and he combines his thanksgiving with words about personal contentment. He wanted the people to know that through all of life's experiences he has learned to be content. With Paul's decision to follow Jesus came a life that certainly had its joy, but it was also one that was filled with trials. He was looked upon with mistrust, continuously persecuted, the victim of assault and imprisonment, and finally martyred for preaching the gospel.

What does it mean to be content with one's life? Contentment can be defined as being satisfied with one's circumstances. But if this is contentment, it does not reflect the lives of most people. Although there is nothing wrong with desiring a better life, some people are on an endless search, trying to meet their emotional needs with activities and possessions. They are looking for meaning and fulfillment with inanimate objects, careers, and anything else the world might offer them. The Roman poet Horace wrote, "Those who want much are always in need. Happy is the person to whom God gives with a sparing hand what is sufficient to their wants." This doesn't sound like our philosophy of life or idea of success.

The great philosophers were searching for the highest truth or ultimate reality. In a state of discontentment, they were seeking the answers that would fill the void in one's life. But Paul learned that contentment is not found in this world or through a philosophical search. Instead, it is found in the person of Jesus Christ. He knew that regardless of where life took him, the Lord was there to meet his needs. His faith and contentment was in the one who paid the penalty for his sins and who conquered death. For Paul, contentment was directly related to the soul, and it becomes a reality when we receive the Spirit of the Risen Christ. Contentment comes to those who let go of material pursuits and walk in the teachings of Jesus.

We live in a world where human value is based upon accomplishments and possessions, to the exclusion of the inner life. The focus is upon what we can receive, rather than what we can give. Paul discovered that the world is often a distraction, pulling us away from the grace and life that God offers us. We get caught up in believing that our status is what makes the difference, when in fact it has nothing to do with who we are as a person. We were created to be in communion with the Lord, and we will only be content when our hearts have been surrendered in faith. Try as we may, we will never experience divine peace until we commit ourselves to God and walk the sacrificial path of Christ.

WHAT IS BEAUTY?

Isaiah 53:1–3

> Who has believed our message, and to whom has the arm of the Lord been revealed? He grew up before him like a tender shoot, and like a root out of dry ground. He had no beauty or majesty to attract us to him, nothing in his

appearance that we should desire him. He was despised and rejected by men, a man of sorrows and familiar with suffering. Like one from whom men hide their faces, he was despised, and we esteemed him not.

Isaiah's words prophetically speak about the Messiah, who came in the person of Jesus Christ. But rather than revealing the glory of God's Son, we see a picture of one coming from a lowly background. Unlike Israel's kings who reigned in worldly splendor, having wealth and power, Isaiah paints a different image of our Savior. Not only do we find an individual without the majesty known to worldly rulers, but we learn that Jesus lacked the physical appearance that would attract us to him. Isaiah wrote that there was nothing in his appearance that would cause a person to take a second look at Jesus. In other words, by the world's standards, Jesus lacked the outer appearance that one would consider handsome and charismatic.

The world defines a beautiful person as someone who is pleasing to the eye, and one who stirs the senses. While there are certainly exceptions, our initial attraction to another person tends to involve their physical appearance. Unfortunately, this has been true throughout history. Why else would Isaiah refer to the Messiah in this manner? The tragedy in these verses is that the world is caught up in the physical senses, not realizing the true meaning of beauty. Can you imagine rejecting God's Son because of his physical appearance? We have our ideas of what Jesus looked like, as if it were important. Churches hang pictures of an individual who is well-groomed and physically fit. Some of these pictures depict a Jesus with long flowing hair, penetrating eyes, and a compassionate expression. But Isaiah reveals that our minds have created the look that we desire.

To know the heart and mind of Jesus is to realize the true meaning of beauty, for it is the soul of a person that reflects who they are. To place physical beauty within the context of human value is to falsify God's Word and the true meaning of life. If beauty relates to the physical, then how are we to understand the aging process? Do we lose our beauty as we mature in years? Although we know the answers to these questions, it does not negate the fact that we get caught up in physical appearances, often to the exclusion of a person's real beauty.

What the world understands as beauty will one day turn to ashes and disappear forever. True beauty is found in Jesus Christ, the one who had nothing in his appearance that we should desire him. The beauty of Christ is found in his pure heart and holy life, which led him to willingly sacrifice his life for us. It is this Spirit in us that brings God's beauty into our lives for others to see and experience.

THE GIFT OF JOY

Galatians 5:19–25

> The acts of the sinful nature are obvious: sexual immorality, impurity and debauchery; idolatry and witchcraft; hatred, discord, jealousy, fits of rage, selfish ambition, dissensions, factions and envy; drunkenness, orgies, and the like. I warn you, as I did before, that those who live like this will not inherit the kingdom of God. But the fruit of the Spirit is love, joy, peace, patience, kindness, goodness, faithfulness, gentleness and self-control. Against such things there is no law. Those who belong to Christ Jesus have crucified the sinful nature with its passions and desires. Since we live by the Spirit, let us keep in step with the Spirit.

In this letter Paul contrasted the life of sin to that of the Spirit, and he exhorted believers to choose the latter or lose their salvation. The gifts of the Holy Spirit are many, and their presence in one's life brings an inner peace and joy that cannot be found in the world. When the soul is at peace with God, a divine joy is the result. With this being true, why do so many Christians lack the gift of joy in their lives? Do we realize some level of joy when we receive Jesus as our Savior, or does this gift only come through spiritual maturity?

Francis Asbury, the first Methodist bishop in the United States, wrote that Christianity cannot exist without peace, love, and joy. He said, "If there is real joy in the world, it is the pure and mature heart that possesses it. When a rusty nail is put into the fire its rust is burned away, and this is what happens to a heart that is put through the fire of Almighty God." According to this belief, the problem relating to joy seems to be the lack of spiritual development and intimacy with the Lord. There is certainly joy when we receive Christ into our lives, but without spiritual growth the trials of life have a way of destroying this joy. Christian joy is dependent upon deep spiritual roots and a growing faith. Paul tells us that when a heart is totally committed to the Lord, there is inner peace and joy. This statement seems to correspond to that of Francis Asbury.

Possessing God's joy, however, does not mean a trouble-free life. There will always be times of struggle, pain, and sorrow, when we are disheartened. Life is full of situations that work against our inner peace. But regardless of the trial, nothing can remove the personal joy of the Spirit within us. Through prayer, continued faith, and commitment, our joy will be kept alive. The life of the Spirit will be held in uninterrupted joy as we continue to walk with the Lord. Even when we are deeply distressed, God promises to give us his peace. In fact, it is during such times that the Holy Spirit becomes our comforter, strength, and source of hope.

John Wesley often spoke about Christian joy. On one occasion he said, "All happiness, in any of its forms, comes from setting our love for the Creator above our love of the creation." When we lack joy, there is a spiritual void in our lives that must honestly and prayerfully be addressed. As we come before the Lord seeking answers, the Holy Spirit will enable us to see ourselves under God's probing light of truth. What matters is how we respond to the Lord's voice. Joy is a gift of the Spirit that develops as we increase in love for God and one another.

RESPONSES TO TRUTH

John 8:42–47

> Jesus said to them, "If God were your Father, you would love me, for I came from God and now am here. I have not come on my own; but he sent me. Why is my language not clear to you? Because you are unable to hear what I say. You belong to your father, the devil, and you want to carry out your father's desire. He was a murderer from the beginning, not holding to the truth, for there is no truth in him. When he lies, he speaks his native language, for he is a liar and the father of lies. Yet because I tell you the truth, you do not believe me! Can any of you prove me guilty of sin? If I am telling the truth, why don't you believe me? He who belongs to God hears what God says. The reason you do not hear is that you do not belong to God."

Prior to this discourse, Jesus received an angry response from a group of people that he confronted with God's truths. These individuals were boasting to Jesus about their lineage, letting him know that they were sons of Abraham, and they did not need to listen to him. Like many people, they expressed a sense of security in another person's righteousness. In verse thirty-seven we have Jesus' response to their claim. He said, "I know you are Abraham's descendants. Yet you are ready to kill me, because you have no room for my word. I am telling you what I have seen in the Father's presence, and you do what you have heard from your father." Jesus made it clear that their father was the devil, who was robbing them of God's grace. He told them that if they were truly Abraham's children they would not be responding to him with such resistance and animosity. They claimed to be religious people, yet they sought to kill God's anointed messenger. Their pride and self-righteousness blinded them to the truth that is in Jesus Christ. Even though they were aware of our Savior's authority and power, they refused to open their hearts and minds to the Spirit's leading. In fact, they used their spiritual lineage as an excuse.

Time has certainly changed many things, but it has not changed the human heart and the responses to the message of salvation. People allow pride to control their sense of reason, which in turn blocks the movement of the Holy Spirit and the grace offered by God. When this happens we are doing the devil's will, which is what Jesus reveals in this passage. This is often done in the name of religion. Jesus emphasizes that we can only serve one master, and a divided life is not the path to salvation. We have a tendency to pick and choose the scripture that we call truth, to the exclusion of passages that convict us of our sins. When God's Word makes us feel uncomfortable, we often try to erase it from our minds.

Paul wrote that all scripture is inspired for the purpose of teaching, rebuking, correcting, and training in righteousness. How do we respond to this statement? Do we really allow the Word to speak to our hearts for the purpose of transformation and spiritual growth? Jesus said that those who belong to God, not only hear the Word, but they apply it to their lives. For example, how can we be serious about our salvation and service to God if we reject the teachings of Christ? If we are not prayerfully grounded in the Word, we will continuously falter in our responses to truth. Only when the love of Jesus changes us, will we be willing to allow God's Word to speak to our hearts.

THE GIFT OF PEACE

John 14:23–27

> Jesus said, "If anyone loves me, he will obey my teachings. My Father will love him, and we will come to him and make our home with him. He who does not love me will not obey my teaching. These words you hear are not my own; they belong to the Father who sent me. All this I have spoken while still with you, but the Counselor, the Holy Spirit, whom the Father will send in my name, will teach you all things and will remind you of everything I have said to you. Peace I leave with you; my peace I give to you. I do not give to you as the world gives. Do not let your hearts be troubled and do not be afraid.

With these reassuring words, Jesus was preparing his apostles for his departure. He knew that this would be a traumatic time for them, and he wanted them to know that they would not be left alone. As they continued to live in his teachings of love and forgiveness, the Holy Spirit would give them strength, comfort, and guidance. Jesus also promised them his peace, which was a gift they certainly needed as they went out to proclaim the gospel.

We have all seen Christmas cards that focus on the word *peace*. Some of these cards read: *May the peace of Christmas be yours; On Christmas, peace came to earth;* and *Peace on earth and goodwill toward men.* These are inspiring words, but many people question whether such peace is possible in this life. It sounds good, but where is this peace that Jesus speaks about? As we read these words the world is in turmoil. It always has been, and there is no indication that things will change. Since the creation of humanity, it seems that violence has removed any possibility of peace in our lives and in the world. There is even division and strife in the Church of Jesus Christ. Every pastor knows how challenging it is to maintain unity and peace in congregations.

What kind of peace did Jesus promise his followers? If this peace does exist, where does it come from, and how is it received? In spite of all the problems in our world, people do want some manner of peace. Even revolutionaries and those who initiate wars often claim that peace is their objective. This, of course, is questionable in some cases. But for the most part, we seek peace in our lives. After all, who desires to live with constant anxiety and strife?

The peace that Jesus offers is not of this world. This makes sense, for we know that our world cannot produce real and lasting peace. Our Savior promises a peace that is given by God through the indwelling presence of the Holy Spirit. It is a reality that comes to those who love God and prayerfully strive to walk in the teachings of Christ. Regardless what we have accomplished or possess, contentment is only experienced by those who have been transformed through their faith and love for God. Clearly stated, our peace is the presence of God in us. It is a peace that passes all human understanding, for it is rooted in the mystery of our Creator.

When we receive the peace of Christ we have both the desire and ability to be at peace with all people, including those whom we perceive to be our enemies. It is the peace within us that makes peace with others possible. As the saying goes, you cannot give what you don't possess. To the church in Ephesus Paul wrote, "With all humility and gentleness and patience, show forbearance to one another in love, being diligent to preserve the unity of the Spirit in the bond of peace."

Thirteen

TRANSFORMING GRACE

WALKING IN THE SPIRIT

Galatians 5:13–18

> You, my brothers, were called to be free. But do not use your freedom to indulge the sinful nature; rather serve one another in love. The entire law is summed up in a single command: "Love your neighbor as yourself." If you keep on biting and devouring each other, watch out or you will be destroyed by each other. So I say, live by the Spirit, and you will not gratify the desires of the sinful nature. For the sinful nature desires what is contrary to the Spirit, and the Spirit what is contrary to the sinful nature. They are in conflict with each other, so that you do not do what you want. But if you are led by the Spirit, you are not under the law.

In these verses the apostle Paul focuses upon both sin and righteousness. It is a comparison of good versus evil, which was a concept familiar to the Greeks, who believed that every person possessed this dual nature. They understood good and evil to be meshed into human nature; therefore, it was impossible to escape from the control of evil forces. Some contemporary theologians adhere to this belief, claiming that there is no freedom from the control of sin.

Paul believed that, although we are sinners, we can be set free from the bondage of sin. Through Jesus Christ and the indwelling power of the Holy Spirit, we can become new people. To deny this, is to say that God has no power for us in the present. If the Lord cannot change people in this life, then his power is limited and his Word is false. If we cannot change in the present, how can we have hope for the future? A life that cannot change is a hopeless existence. Paul affirms that our spiritual regeneration is through the Holy Spirit, who convicts us of our unrighteousness and provides the strength to resist temptation and sin.

Paul tells us to rejoice, because God can set us free from the chains of sin. Regardless of our imperfections and weaknesses, we can have a pure heart that enables us to love God and humanity. Living in the Spirit is victory over the sins of pride, self-centeredness, hatred, and revenge. Rather than a state of spiritual perfection, it is freedom from the control of sin. When Jesus is our Lord and Savior the condition of our heart changes, which is a transformation Paul refers to as the circumcision of the heart. It is a spiritual surgery that results in the fruits of the Spirit, all of which manifest a pure and gentle heart that seeks to glorify the Lord. The new life given by God involves the whole person, including the will, feelings, intellect, and actions.

Paul wrote the Galatians that those who belong to Christ have crucified the desires and passions of the sinful nature. They live a life that seeks to please God and serve others in the example given to us by Jesus. This, of course, is a sanctifying process in which growth is ongoing. As we remain faithful and committed to God, our relationship with him deepens. By allowing the Spirit to control our life, God continues to reveal more of himself to us. As such, we become more cognizant of our nature and purpose.

The Lord has sent us the Light of his Spirit to restore the humanity that was lost to sin. But are we opening ourselves up to the Light? Are we willing to allow the Spirit to take control of our life? God has taken the initiative to transform us, and to show us the way. What is our response to the Lord's initiative?

LIVING IN THE PRESENT

James 4:13–17

> Now listen, you who say, "Today or tomorrow we will go to this or that city, spend a year there, carry on business and make money." Why, you do not even know what will happen tomorrow. What is your life? You are a mist that appears for a little while and then vanishes. Instead, you ought to say, "If it is the Lord's will we will live and do this or that." As it is, you boast and brag. All such boasting is evil. Anyone, then, who knows the good he ought to do and doesn't do it, sins.

We have a tendency to look at our lives either in the past or future. In fact, we sometimes do this to such an extent that there is a void in the present.

This directly affects God's unfolding plan for us, which involves how the Lord desires to use us each day. In his epistle to the Christian community, James wrote about the importance of living in the present. He told his readers that no one knows what the future holds; therefore, our concern must be each day that the Lord gives us.

Everyone knows how life can drastically change in a matter of seconds. Regardless of how well we plan for the future, there are no guarantees. The loss of employment, health, family issues, or death, can suddenly change the direction of the future. Who can predict the future, when we do not even know what will happen before the end of the day. This means that every minute is of the utmost importance in serving God and one another. Although it is not wrong to plan for the future, we must make the present our priority. To live outside of the present is to remove God from our lives.

To emphasize these truths, James asked, "What is your life?" He then answered this question by saying that we are a mist that only appears for a short while. This graphic imagery opens our eyes to the brevity of life, as well as the uncertainty of the future. It addresses our priorities by stressing the good that we should do today, knowing that opportunities vanish. James wrote, "Anyone who knows the good he ought to do and doesn't do it, sins." This is a strong statement that speaks to the importance of living each day for the Lord.

Jesus told his disciples not to worry about the future, for each day carries enough concerns. He also said that tomorrow will take care of itself. This, however, requires a level of faith that many people lack. The apostle Paul teaches that faith is not merely a profession, but rather a life that is lived each day. Jesus told his followers that they must work and do good while it is daylight. In other words, they were to take advantage of their time and God-given opportunities. This is difficult for people who yearn for the past or look to the future as a better place to be. The Lord presents himself to us every day, but we fail to hear his voice when we are not focused upon the present.

After serving in the military and having had a career in both law enforcement and the ministry, I have constantly been reminded of the brevity and uncertainty of life. These reminders have changed my priorities and how I approach each day. It has led me to pray daily for God's will and leading. The Lord seeks to use our time, talents, possessions, and experiences to bring others into his world of forgiveness and grace. As we approach each new day, how often do we pray for enlightenment and the leading of the Holy Spirit? Every day is an opportunity for personal growth and service.

UNFAILING LOVE

I Corinthians 15:9, 10

> For I am the least of the apostles and do not even deserve to be called an apostle, because I persecuted the church of God. But by the grace of God I am what I am, and his grace to me was not without effect. No, I worked harder than all of them—yet not I, but the grace of God that was with me. Whether, then, it was I or they, this is what we preach, and this is what you believe.

The apostle Paul wanted the Corinthians to know that we serve a God of infinite mercy, and he uses himself as an example. Paul claims to have been the worst of sinners, admitting that he aggressively persecuted the early Church. But God's grace transformed him, saving the one whose mission was to destroy the gospel message. The Lord poured out his mercy on the one who stood by and watched as Stephen was stoned to death. Christians initially feared Paul, but through the love and power of Jesus Christ he became a great apostle, theologian, and evangelist. He sacrificed his entire life and was eventually martyred for his faith and mission work.

Regardless of what sins we have committed, the Lord never gives up on us. His unfailing and transforming grace is always present, seeking to save us from ourselves. When we think about giving up on others, we should remember God's patience toward us. Paul is an excellent example of how God's grace can change one's heart and direction in life. It was an encounter with Jesus Christ that convinced Paul of his sins, bringing him into God's saving grace. What a truth for us, for God's grace is available to everyone enslaved in sin. Over the years I experienced this truth with many individuals, especially during my tenure as a state prison chaplain. The presence of God during one's darkest hour was revealed to me when I was the pastor for an execution. In the midst of the agony preceding the execution, came a divine peace that brought hope to the inmate. It was a peace that was experienced by everyone who was present.

Some people, however, say that the grace given to Paul was different because the Spirit of the risen Christ actually spoke to him on the road to Damascus. But isn't it true that the Spirit of the risen Christ continues to speak to people today. One may not hear an audible voice, but there is no doubt when the Holy Spirit speaks to our hearts, convicting us of sin and offering forgiving grace and reconciliation with God. It is divine grace that removes the scales from our eyes, enabling us to see the truth that is found in Jesus Christ. Paul said, "By the grace of God I am what I am." It is our response to the Holy Spirit that brings transformation and molds us into the image of Christ.

For Paul to become a servant of the Lord, he had to rid himself of pride and step out in faith. Only then could he internalize and live in God's grace, and the same is true for us. When we take this step, we can say with Paul that we are who we are by the grace of God. Regardless of where we are in life, the Lord's compassion and mercy is always present.

CLOUDED VISION

Luke 6:41–48

> Jesus said, "Why do you look at the speck of sawdust in your brother's eye and pay no attention to the plank in your own eye? How can you say to your brother, 'Brother, let me take the speck out of your eye,' when you yourself fail to see the plank in your own eye? You hypocrite, first take the plank out of your eye, and then you will see clearly to remove the speck from your brother's eye."

Jesus uses the simplest illustrations to communicate the most profound truths. In this passage of scripture he speaks about specks of sawdust and planks of wood. Since his earthly father was a carpenter, these images were a part of his life. What is interesting is that he is using them to share truths about humanity. How we see things directly relates to our spiritual life, and this includes our understanding of people. Those with a pure heart refrain from judging others, primarily because they are aware of their own imperfections and sins. It is easy to see the sins of other people, but not the magnitude of our own sins. This is the comparison between the speck of sawdust and the plank that Jesus is speaking about.

When we honestly examine our lives, we tend to be less judgmental of others. How can we condemn others when we ourselves are sinners in need of continuous grace? We so often look at others through the eyes of envy, prejudice, or resentment, all of which is sin. When our vision is blurred it is impossible to see the good in other people, and this directly impacts upon our spirituality and our ability to witness to our faith. Instead of enabling others to see God in us, thereby drawing people to Jesus, our lack of love and understanding does the opposite. In a sense, we are hypocrites of the life that we profess, to the detriment of those around us. Can you imagine if the Lord condemned us, rather than offering us hope and a new life?

Jesus tells us that if we wish to see clearly, we must remove the plank that is clouding our vision. This means honestly looking at our own heart and life, both past and present. It is a humbling experience to examine ourselves in the light of God's Word and grace. When doing this, we realize that it is only by the mercy of God that we have been forgiven. When we reflect upon our infirmities and sins, the speck of sawdust in another person's eye suddenly disappears. This allows us to see people through the clear vision of our Savior. But people would rather judge others than themselves, for it is too painful to look at oneself. Self-examination brings God's conviction, and this is not the desire of many people.

The Lord wants us to have clear vision, but this requires a pure heart that is filled with the love of Christ. When it comes to our spiritual life, it is the heart that determines how we see other people. Therefore, it is the heart through which we become witnesses and servants of the Lord. We should walk through life with the knowledge that we are only forgiven through God's grace. Living with this truth improves our vision, and this is when we begin to see individuals through the compassionate eyes of Jesus.

A HEALING AND A WARNING

John 5:1–9, 14

> Some time later, Jesus went up to Jerusalem for a feast of the Jews. Now there is in Jerusalem near the Sheep Gate a pool, which in Aramaic is called Bethesda, which is surrounded by five covered colonnades. Here a great number of disabled people used to lie—the blind, the lame, the paralyzed. One who was there, had been an invalid for thirty-eight years. When Jesus saw him lying there and learned that he had been in this condition for a long time, he asked him, "Do you want to get well?" "Sir," the invalid replied, "I have no one to help me into the pool when the water is stirred. While I am trying to get in, someone else goes down ahead of me." Then Jesus said to him, "Get up! Pick up you mat and walk." At once the man was cured; he picked up his mat and walked. Later, Jesus found him in the temple and said to him, "See, you are well again. Stop sinning or something worse may happen to you."

The pool referred to by the apostle John was located by archaeologists in 1888. The remains were found near the Sheep Gate, with what appears to be evidence of five arched porticoes. The word Bethesda means *House of Mercy*, which was a befitting name for this pool. The water was known for its medicinal properties, especially during certain times. It was believed that an angel of the Lord stirred up the waters, causing a bubbling effect that brought healing power.

The man in our story was in a hopeless state, having suffered from an infirmity for thirty-eight years. Although we do not know what caused his condition, there was no medical cure that could heal him. This pool of mercy was his last hope, but no one would carry him to its healing waters. Jesus knew that the man had been disabled for many years, and he asked him if he wanted to get well. What a strange question to ask someone who was making every effort to enter the healing waters of the pool. We can only believe that Jesus was testing the man's will and leading him to examine his spiritual life. The Lord speaks to the human heart, asking us if we really desire spiritual healing. Do we desire to be cleansed from the disease of sin. If so, how much determination and faith do we possess?

There were many people around the pool of Bethesda, but this particular man was undoubtedly one of the worst cases. If Jesus could cure him, then there was certainly hope for others. It is interesting that Jesus did not take the man to the pool for healing. Instead, he simply told the man to pick up his mat and walk. Those who witnessed this miracle would certainly know that Jesus possessed divine power. Like his words on love and forgiveness, his healings opened a door for the message of salvation.

The paralyzed man was given a new life that was rooted in the compassion and mercy of Christ. In his hopeless state, he was confronted with the only one who could cure his disease. Even though the law forbade someone to carry a mat on the Sabbath, he followed the command of Jesus. In his excitement, he even told others of Jesus' healing power. As you noted, Jesus told the man to stop sinning or something worse would happen to him. This was a statement that our spiritual healing takes precedence over our physical needs. Although the Lord is concerned about our physical health, nothing is more important than our forgiveness and eternal destiny.

Fourteen

DELIVERANCE AND RENEWAL

THE NEW COVENANT

Jeremiah 31:31–34

> "The time is coming," declares the Lord, "when I will make a new covenant with the house of Israel and with the house of Judah. It will not be like the covenant I made with their forefathers when I took them by the hand to lead them out of Egypt, because they broke my covenant, though I was a husband to them," declares the Lord. "This is the covenant I will make with the house of Israel after that time," declares the Lord. "I will put my law in their minds, and write it in their hearts. I will be their God, and they will be my people. No longer will a man teach his neighbor, or a man his brother, saying, 'Know the Lord,' because they will all know me, from the least of them to the greatest," declares the Lord. "For I will forgive their wickedness and will remember their sins no more."

These prophetic words uttered by the prophet Jeremiah speak about a New Covenant being prepared by God that would change the meaning of the Law. It was to be a covenant that focused upon one's spiritual regeneration, emphasizing a personal relationship with the Lord. Rather than the people ritualistically obeying the Law, the Word of God would somehow be inscribed into their minds and hearts. In this new agreement, God promised to live within the heart of every person of faith. The Lord also spoke about forgiving one's sins apart from the law and animal sacrifices. Through a person's contrite heart and life of faith, God would forgive the sins of the people.

This was a strange prophecy that Jeremiah communicated, for the Jews lived under the Levitical system of laws and sacrifices. It was a system that was supposed to bring accountability and responsibility, while leading the people to a life committed to God. Just as the entire animal was sacrificed to the Lord, God required that each person offer themselves as living sacrifices. The unblemished sacrifices were a graphic spiritual message to the Israelites.

The prophecy of Joel was true when he said that one day the Spirit of God would be poured out upon all people. In God's timing, Jesus was to bring God's New Covenant to the people through his sacrifice on the cross. No longer would the people sacrifice animals, for their forgiveness would come through the one sacrifice of Christ. Rather than simply possessing knowledge and uncertain hope, everyone who received Jesus Christ would be assured of their salvation.

This was the prophecy that God gave to Jeremiah, which had its fulfillment in the life, death, and resurrection of Jesus. It is a message of certain hope for all who surrender their lives to God through the atoning work of Christ. This prophecy, which fell upon deaf ears, was the good news of God. Jesus has promised to write his law of love upon our hearts and to remember our sins no more. The Old Covenant had its purpose, but it is only through the circumcision of the heart that we become righteous before God.

As we examine our lives, have we received the New Covenant made possible through the blood of Jesus Christ? Jesus said, "Come to me, all you who are weary and burdened, and I will give you rest. Take my yoke upon you and learn from me, for I am gentle and humble in heart, and you will find rest for your souls."

SAVING BY LOSING

Matthew 16:24–26

> Then Jesus said to his disciples, "If anyone would come after me, he must deny himself and take up his cross and follow me. For whoever wants to save his life will lose it, but whoever loses his life for me will find it. What good will it be for a man if he gains the whole world, yet forfeits his soul? Or what can a man give in exchange for his soul?"

Jesus told his disciples that whoever tries to keep their life will lose it. This statement obviously does not reflect human reasoning and logic. It is the antithesis of secular teaching and therefore foreign to our philosophy of life. But much of what Jesus teaches is of this nature, for he wants us to focus upon the soul and eternal realities. On a particular occasion, as Jesus was preparing his apostles for his death, he said to them, "The hour has come for the Son of Man to be glorified. I tell you the truth, unless a kernel of wheat falls into the ground and dies, it remains only a single seed. But if it dies, it produces many seeds. The man who loves his life will lose it, while the man who hates his life in this world will keep it for eternal life." Jesus is using figurative language here to explain how death can be a catalyst for life. In nature, it is the death of a seed that brings new life, and the same truth applies to our spiritual life. It is the death of the old life of pride and self-centeredness that enables our spiritual birth and new life in Christ.

We are called to die to the old life of sin that we might be sown into the life of Jesus Christ. Like the seed given to the soil, our spiritual birth begins a growth process that multiplies and recycles. As we continue to grow in Christ the old self continues to die, bringing forth the beauty of new life. Like a farmer who commits seed to the soil, we commit our lives to Jesus Christ, with the certainty of an inner transformation and certain hope. Countless people have given their lives to worldly pleasures and ambitions, only to be disappointed. We, however, know that our surrender will reap the gifts of the Holy Spirit. This does not suggest a life that lacks hardships, but it does mean that whatever the difficulty, we will continue to grow in the image of our Savior. When we marry, the labor of love begins, and this is true with our marriage to Christ.

For a seed to germinate and a plant to grow, it must remain in the soil and be nurtured by the sun and rain. Our soil is holy ground, and we are nurtured through the Word and the washing away of sin through God's forgiveness. As in nature, spiritual nurturing develops the strong roots that enable us to endure the storms of life. Those who remain rooted in Jesus possess the resources to be strong in the face of adversity.

To lose oneself to the Lord also means giving yourself to others. It is to see all people as God's children, with whom Jesus seeks a relationship. Life is no longer centered upon ourselves, for the Holy Spirit calls us to a world of human need and suffering. This is the life that brings eternal blessings, for when we live the sacrificial life of Christ, we receive the Lord's blessings.

THE NEW BIRTH

John 3:1–6

> Now there was a man of the Pharisees named Nicodemus, a member of the Jewish ruling council. He came to Jesus at night and said, "Rabbi, we know

that you are a teacher who has come from God. For no one could perform the miraculous signs you are doing if God were not with him." In reply Jesus declared, "I tell you the truth, unless a man is born again, he cannot see the kingdom of God." "How can a man be born when he is old?" Nicodemus asked. "Surely he cannot enter a second time into his mother's womb to be born!" Jesus answered, "I tell you the truth, unless a man is born of the water and the Spirit, he cannot enter the kingdom of God. Flesh gives birth to flesh, but the Spirit gives birth to spirit."

In some Christian circles the words *born again* have a negative connotation, but these are the words that Jesus used when speaking to Nicodemus. Although Nicodemus was an educated and pious teacher of the law, he was impressed with Jesus, believing that he was a man sent by God. The word "we" seems to indicate that there were others in Nicodemus' circle who were also impressed with Jesus. Because Nicodemus saw Jesus as an inspired and anointed teacher, he came to him for an understanding of God's kingdom. Our Savior knew that his nightly visitor had questions about salvation, and before Nicodemus could make an inquiry, Jesus told him that he must be born again. But our Lord's statement confused this religious leader, whom the people saw as a spiritual guide.

Jesus wanted Nicodemus to know that simply being born a Jew and having biblical knowledge was not the path to salvation. Nor were traditions, rituals, and meticulous adherence to the law enough to enter God's kingdom. Jesus emphasized that a spiritual birth was necessary for one to be reconciled with God. While we can assume that Nicodemus felt he was missing something, this is not to say that our Lord's response gave him immediate clarification.

John Wesley made a comparison between a natural and spiritual birth. He said that in the womb there is darkness and confinement. The baby's physical senses are not developed, and there are limits relating to physical growth. But at birth, a child enters the world of physical light and is set free from the darkness of the womb. It is now that development and life can truly begin. Before being born of God, we find similar comparisons. When our birth in Christ occurs, we are set free to experience all that God intends for us. Everything around us takes on a new dimension and meaning, as we begin to experience the Spirit within us.

Our new birth results in a new person, for it begins a sanctifying process that puts to death the old life of sin and bondage. It is analogous to a new home that is built with a strong foundation and new building materials. Jesus Christ is the cornerstone of our new structure, and through him we bear the spiritual fruit that continues to change us. Nicodemus knew that he was missing something, and he was given the answer to his question!

FROM DEATH TO LIFE
Ephesians 2:1–10

> As for you, you were dead in your transgressions and sins, in which you use to live when you followed the ways of the world and the ruler of the kingdom of the air, the spirit who is now at work in those who are disobedient. All of us, also lived among them at one time, gratifying the cravings of our sinful nature and following its desires and thoughts. Like the rest, we were by nature objects of wrath. But because of his great love for us, God, who is rich in mercy, made us alive with Christ, even when we were dead in transgressions—it is by grace you have been saved. And God raised us up with Christ and seated us with him in the heavenly realms in Christ Jesus, in order that in the coming ages he might show the incomparable riches of his grace, expressed in his kindness to us in Christ Jesus. For it is by grace that you have been saved, through faith—and this is not from yourselves, it is the gift of God—not by works, so that no one can boast. For we are God's workmanship, created in Christ Jesus to do good works, which God prepared in advance for us to do.

Spiritual death can be compared to a dark tunnel, in which you continuously hear the echo of your unrepentant life. It is that darkness of the soul when you are far away from the Lord. The apostle Paul experienced this when he cried out, "O wretched man that I am, who will deliver me from this body of death?" Paul had all the privileges, both worldly comfort and influential power. As an educated Pharisee, he also had religion and knowledge of the law. In fact, his beliefs were such that he became a militant defender of fundamental Judaism, while at the same time persecuting the followers of Jesus Christ. But Paul was a misguided zealot and legalist, who eventually realized that his religion had killed his soul. He was walking in the shadows of eternal death, until confronted by the risen Jesus. What an awesome awakening when God shakes our spiritual foundations. Paul became aware that he was separated from the Lord and in need of forgiveness and restoration.

To be spiritually restored is to be reconciled with God and to know the joy of salvation. Restoration impacts upon every area of life, changing one's perceptions and direction. It affects the whole person, thereby changing our relationships. In essence, it is being at peace with God and all creation. Paul discovered that religion does not change the inner person. Ritual and meticulous adherence to the law did not change Paul's heart and offer him hope. Although the Lord continuously warned Israel about their legalistic ways and the need for inner transformation, they were slow learners. Paul was a product of a religious system that smothered the work of the Spirit.

Baptism is a practiced sacrament with most Christian churches. With an infant, it is God's seal of restoration and salvation based solely upon divine grace. Children remain in this state until they reach the age of accountability, when they must act upon their free will and make a decision. For adults, baptism is also an outer sign of an inner working of grace. However, with adults it involves repentance and personal faith in Jesus Christ. But regardless of whether the baptism involves an infant or adult, it is the regenerating power of the Holy Spirit that brings us into a relationship with God. This transition from death to life is one that begins and continues through divine grace and personal faith.

VICTORY OVER DEATH

I Corinthians 15:50–58

> I declare to you brothers that flesh and blood cannot inherit the kingdom of God, nor does the perishable inherit the imperishable. Listen, I tell you a mystery: We will not all sleep, but we will all be changed—in a flash, in the twinkling of an eye, at the last trumpet. For the trumpet will sound, the dead will be raised imperishable, and we will be changed. For the perishable must clothe itself with the imperishable, and the mortal with immortality. When the perishable has been clothed with the imperishable, and the mortal with immorality, then the saying that is written will come true: "Death has been swallowed up in victory." "Where, O death, is your victory? Where, O death, is your sting?" The sting of death is sin, and the power of sin is the law. But thanks be to God! He gives us the victory through our Lord Jesus Christ. Therefore, my dear brothers, stand firm. Let nothing move you. Always give yourselves fully to the work of the Lord, because you know that your labor in the Lord is not in vain.

In this writing the apostle Paul encouraged the believers in Corinth to remain strong in their faith, knowing that their commitment to Jesus Christ will bring them victory over death. It was not physical death that Paul was speaking about, but rather spiritual death. He wanted the Corinthians to think about death as a passage into God's glorious and eternal realm. But to experience God's kingdom they must remain faithful, trusting in the atoning work and promises of Christ. During times of persecution, Paul knew that the followers of Christ were anxious about death. Were the promises of Jesus true? If so, would they have the strength and courage to trust in those promises?

Although death is as common as birth, people have a difficult time seeing the parallels. While the birth of someone is celebrated, funerals bring sadness and a deep sense of loss. But just as we prepare for a new physical birth within the family, we are also to make preparation for our death and eternal future. The thought of one's death unleashes many emotions, which include anxiety and fear. While we often prepare for death by purchasing insurance policies and cemetery plots, little time is given to one's spiritual preparation. I have known individuals who wrote their own obituary, making certain that their accomplishments were told. These same individuals, however, never mentioned God during their last days and hours. Although worldly preparations are necessary, they will not change our destiny. Most people claim to believe in an afterlife, but they deny it by not preparing themselves for their eternal future.

Paul wrote the Corinthians that the sting of death is sin, which includes trying to find salvation through the law and good works. But he said, "Thanks be to God! He gives us the victory through our Lord Jesus Christ." Paul urged believers to stand firm in their commitment by giving themselves fully to the Lord's work. By doing so, they would not only experience God's power and glory in the present, but their victory over death was assured. He said that on the last day the dead in Christ will rise first, and those who are living will be raptured and transformed. This is the victory promised to all who remain faithful. We must examine our lives in light of God's Word. Are we standing firm in our Christian walk, not allowing any person or situation to take our eyes off of Jesus, the one who gives us victory? Do you have the witness of the Spirit that you have already passed from death to life?

RAISING JAIRUS' DAUGHTER

Mark 5:21–24, 35–42

> While he was by the lake, one of the synagogue rulers, named Jairus, came there. Seeing Jesus, he fell at his feet and pleaded earnestly with him, "My little daughter is dying. Please come and put your hands on her so that she will be healed and live." Some men came from the house of Jairus, saying, "Your daughter is dead. Why bother the teacher any more?" Ignoring what they said, Jesus told the synagogue ruler, "Don't be afraid, just believe." He did not let anyone follow him except Peter, James and John the brother of James. When

they came to the home of the synagogue ruler, Jesus saw commotion, with people crying and wailing loudly. He went in and said to them, "Why all this commotion and wailing? The child is not dead but asleep." But they laughed at him. After he put them all out, he took the child's father and mother and the disciples who were with him, and went in where the child was. He took her by the hand and said to her, "Little girl, I say to you, get up!" Immediately the girl stood up and walked around (she was twelve years old). After this they were completely astonished. He gave them strict orders not to let anyone know about this, and told them to give her something to eat.

In my second year of ministry I experienced the saddest day of my life. Late one evening a tornado went through my parish, resulting in the death of two young girls from separate families. One of the girls was ten, and the other was twelve years old. I cannot explain the depth of sorrow that gripped our church family and how helpless I felt. In their distress and sorrow, the parents of one of the girls tore at my clothing when her body was viewed at the hospital.

Our text first reveals a father's pain over his sick and dying child, only to learn that she had taken her last breath. There seemed to be some hope while the girl was still alive, but when the announcement came of her death, that hope suddenly ended. The men who reported the girl's death to Jairus, said, "Your daughter is dead. Why bother the teacher any more?" At this point the people had not yet understood who Jesus was. They may have heard about some of his miracles, but what person has power over death? As the men said, there was no reason to pursue the matter any longer. Jesus, however, ignored what they said, telling Jairus to have faith and not to fear.

When Jesus came to the home of the synagogue ruler he was confronted with commotion and people wailing. The pain of this young girl's death was too much for them to bear, and they could not restrain their emotions. In the midst of their wailing Jesus shocked them by saying, "The child is not dead but asleep." This seemingly insensitive remark caused some of the people to laugh at Jesus, for they certainly knew that life had passed from her. Our Savior's response was not meant to undermine the pain and loss, but rather to bring assurance and hope. It was not only a statement about the present situation, but also one that spoke to the eternal state of the soul. This statement was a prelude to what the people would now witness, the raising of Jairus' daughter from the dead.

What was believed to be the end of life and the preparation for a funeral, turned out to be a celebration of life and renewed hope. In Jesus they saw the power of life over death, and they were filled with joy. Never again would they fear the end of this life, for they knew that in Jesus there is resurrection and eternal life. They now understood death as a necessary transition into God's eternal realm.

DELIVERED OF DEMON POSSESSION

Mark 5:1–10

> They went across the lake to the region of Gerasenes. When Jesus got out of the boat, a man with an evil spirit came from the tombs to meet him. This man lived in the tombs, and no one could bind him any more, not even with a chain. For he had often been chained hand and foot, but he tore the chains apart and broke the irons on his feet. No one was strong enough to subdue him. Night and day among the tombs and in the hills he would cry out and cut himself with stones. When he saw Jesus from a distance, he ran and fell on his knees in front of him. He shouted at the top of his voice, "What do you want with me, Jesus, Son of the Most High God? Swear to God that you won't torture me!" For Jesus was saying to him, "Come out of this man, you evil spirit!" Then Jesus asked him, "What is your name?" "My name is Legion," he replied, "for we are many." And he begged Jesus again and again not to send them out of the area.

Mark tells us about a man who was demon possessed. In fact, we learn that he was possessed by a legion of evil spirits. During the time of Christ a Roman army legion comprised at least three thousand men, and at certain times it could be twice that many. This tortured man was living among the tombs, crying out in pain, and cutting his body with sharp stones. The tombs were located outside the city, being a place where criminals and the insane often took refuge. The sepulchers afforded them both shelter and retreat from the weather and the authorities.

Humanly speaking, this was a hopeless situation, for there is no worldly power that can deliver someone from the torture of demonic possession. This man was controlled by evil forces that gave him extraordinary strength. No restraint could subdue him, not even the chains locked around his hands and feet. He was out of control, and a threat to both himself and to others. The demons had taken over his life, and restoration was only possible through exorcism.

The possessed man saw Jesus from a distance, and he fell on his knees in front of him. The evil within him shuddered, knowing that Jesus had the power of expulsion. As in this situation, God's all-encompassing light sees the evil within every person, and he alone has the power to remove it. The demonic presence within the man asked, "What do you want with me, Jesus, Son of the Most High God?" This was a fearful response, for Jesus came into the world to confront every manner of evil.

Our Savior knows the hopelessness of those who are controlled by sin, and how their lives impact upon others. But evil can have such a grip over one's spirit that submission is frequently the result. People continue to resist God's love and power, and this opens the door to every manner of sin. Even though evil results in extreme pain and despair, pride often keeps people from God's grace. We see this truth everywhere, along with the destruction that it causes.

Mark reveals that Jesus rescued the man from demonic possession, an act that amazed onlookers. People asked each other, "What is this? A new teaching—and with authority! He even gives orders to evil spirits, and they obey him." This is the Jesus who is our Lord and Savior, the Son of the Most High God. He has the power to deliver everyone from the control of evil. All we need to do is come before him in humility and faith, allowing his presence to fill our lives.

Fifteen

MIRACLES AND SIGNS

MORE THAN ENOUGH

Mark 6:35–44

> By this time it was late in the day, so his disciples came to him. "This is a remote place," they said, "and it's already late. Send the people away so they can go to the surrounding countryside and villages and buy themselves something to eat." But he answered them, "You give them something to eat." They said to him, "That would take eight months of a man's wages! Are we to go and spend that much on bread and give it to them to eat?" "How many loaves do you have?" he asked. "Go and see." When they found out, they said, "Five—and two fish." Then Jesus directed them to have all the people sit down in groups on the green grass. So they sat down in groups of hundreds and fifties. Taking the five loaves and the two fish and looking up to heaven, he gave thanks and broke the loaves. Then he gave them to his disciples to set before the people. He also divided the two fish among them all. They all ate and were satisfied, and the disciples picked up twelve basketfuls of broken pieces of bread and fish. The number of men who had eaten was five thousand.

We often find Jesus in isolated places that were far from towns and provisions. Mark tells us that Jesus and his disciples were in such a place, with a large group of people who had traveled to listen to his teachings. We can be assured that they knew of the miracles he was known to perform, and that they came either for a physical cure or to see a miracle. Jesus may have even planned this situation for the purpose of revealing God's glory.

It was late in the day, and the people were both weary and hungry. As such, something had to be done, and the disciples voiced their concern to Jesus. They wanted the people to disperse and find rest and food in the surrounding villages. This was certainly a reasonable suggestion, but Jesus had something else in mind. He told his disciples that they should feed the people, which was impossible given the small amount of food that they had. The disciples could not understand why Jesus would ask such a thing, for he was aware of the lack of food. How could five thousand people be fed with just five loaves of bread and two fish?

It seems obvious that Jesus intended to miraculously multiply the food, but he first put his disciples to the test. Would they look to him for a miracle, believing that he had the power? When this did not occur, Jesus met the needs of the large crowd, knowing that they had traveled far from the surrounding villages. Can you imagine the look on the disciples' faces when he told them to bring the loaves and fish to him?

Do we ever question the compassion and power of Jesus? He offers us spiritual food and rest, but we often go away empty and overburdened. As Jesus multiplied the loaves and fish, he will also satisfy our needs by multiplying what is available to us. Paul told the Philippians that God supplies all of our needs, according to his riches in Jesus Christ. The food that Jesus gave the people was free, and it was given to them where they were. There was no need to travel or be concerned about cost. This truth also applies to our salvation and God's continuing grace. The Lord meets us where we are in life, simply asking us to have faith in his abundant mercy and power.

SHOW ME A MIRACLE

Mark 8:11–13

> The Pharisees came and began to question Jesus. To test him, they asked him for a sign from heaven. He sighed deeply and said, "Why does this generation ask for a miraculous sign? I tell you the truth, no sign will be given to it." Then he left them, got back into the boat and crossed to the other side.

The incident that Mark records is found in all four Gospel writings. The question posed by the Pharisees was familiar to Jesus, for his divinity was always questioned. This was true during our Savior's ministry, and it is true today. People want Jesus to prove that he is the Son of God by performing miraculous signs. Some individuals even seek breathtaking and cosmic events to help satisfy their doubts. After all, seeing is believing! The question is, how many miracles must Jesus perform and, of what magnitude, before people will believe?

The Pharisees wanted something spectacular, a clear sign from heaven. They had their own ideas what God must do to prove his presence in Jesus Christ. They set the rules and wanted the Lord to perform for them. Jesus walked away from these self-righteous men, for God will not be manipulated or put to the test. The Lord does not need to prove himself to anyone. The Alpha and the Omega, the Creator and Sustainer of the universe, does not respond to the commands of humanity.

When it comes to miracles, we forget that God is the source and sustenance of all life. The sun is ninety-eight million miles from earth, yet its light, heat, and energy reach us in a matter of minutes. If the sun were a little closer to us, our planet would burn up. If it were farther away, earth would be frozen and lifeless. The moon revolves around the earth in twenty-seven days, seven hours and forty-three minutes, controlling the ocean's tides. There is also the rainfall and the earth's rich soil, which enables us to grow crops and sustain life. All of these realities are miracles that reveal the presence of God.

The Lord is not just the Creator, but also the sustainer of all his precious gifts. Like the precision of a fine-tuned clock, the world is one miracle after another, but it takes spiritual eyes to find God in our daily living. Those who walk in darkness will never see the miraculous presence of the Almighty. Many of God's wonders are found in the familiar things of life that people take for granted; therefore, we need to stop and smell the roses, taking in the wonders of this beautiful creation.

Although the world reveals the mighty works of God, the greatest miracle is found in Jesus Christ. During our Savior's ministry people witnessed his miraculous power, which included raising the dead. It was his own resurrection, however, that brings certain hope to all who receive him in faith. Through the witness and indwelling presence of the Holy Spirit, we have God's assurance of our salvation. It is through the Spirit that we have been changed, giving us the desire and ability to love God and all people. The greatest miracle is our new life in Jesus Christ.

UNSEEN REALITIES

II Kings 6:6–17

> Now the king of Aram was at war with Israel. After conferring with his officers, he said, "I will set up my camp in such and such a place." The man of God sent word to the king of Israel: "Beware of passing that place, because the Arameans

are going down there." So the king of Israel checked on the place indicated by the man of God. Time and again Elisha warned the king, so that he was on his guard in such places. This enraged the king of Aram. He summoned his officers and demanded of them, "Will you not tell me which of us is on the side of the king of Israel?" "None of us, my lord the king," said one of his officers, "but Elisha, the prophet who is in Israel, tells the king of Israel the very words you speak in your bedroom." "Go find out where he is," the king ordered, "so I can send men and capture him." The report came back: "He is in Dothan." Then he sent horses and chariots and a strong force there. They went by night and surrounded the city. When the servant of the man of God got up and went out early the next morning, an army with horses and chariots had surrounded the city. "Oh, my lord, what shall we do?" the servant asked. "Don't be afraid," the prophet answered. "Those who are with us are more than those who are with them." And Elisha prayed, "O Lord, open his eyes so that he may see." The Lord opened the servant's eyes, and he looked and saw the hills full of horses and chariots of fire all around Elisha.

The weapons of God's servants are unseen by the world, for it takes spiritual eyes to see spiritual realities and warfare. It was Elisha's spiritual sight that saved the king of Israel and his forces, and this occurred many times. We are told that time and again Elisha warned the king of impending danger. Through his faith and prayers, Elisha was able to see things that were invisible to others. But when the army was surrounding the city, Elisha's servant was struck with fear and hopelessness. He did not see the forces of God that were preparing for battle.

What a powerful insight for us, for it gives assurance of God's presence during our struggles. Like Job, who did not realize that God was in the midst of his trials, we sometimes feel that the Lord is nowhere to be found. But those of faith possess a power that is unknown to the world. It is the power of experiencing God's spiritual forces watching over them, and this brings assurance. As the apostle Paul learned, it is when we are weak and fearful that the power of God is manifested in its fullness. What makes this possible are eyes of faith, trusting in the Lord's abiding presence. Elisha said to his servant, "Don't be afraid. Those who are with us are more than those who are with them." The apostle John echoed similar words when he wrote, "The one who is in you is greater than the one who is in the world." Didn't Jesus tell us that there were more than twelve legions of angels at his bidding?

Paul said that the natural person lacks the things of the Spirit, and Jesus taught that such people have eyes, but they cannot see spiritual things. They are unable to discern God's presence and the messengers that he sends into their life. No amount of worldly knowledge can do the work of the Holy

Spirit, who opens our eyes to visions of power and hope. When Elisha's servant saw God's powerful army, his fear was removed. Regardless of what we are going through, it is faith and prayer that empowers us to experience the Lord's all-sufficient grace. Those who live in Christ are never outside of God's love and care. Think of your darkest hours, and how the Lord gave you his strength and refuge.

SEEKING MIRACULOUS SIGNS

Matthew 12:38–41

> Then some of the Pharisees and teachers of the law said to him, "Teacher, we want to see miraculous signs from you." He answered, "A wicked and adulterous generation asks for a miraculous sign! But none will be given it except the sign of the prophet Jonah. For as Jonah was three days and three nights in the belly of a huge fish, so the Son of Man will be three days and three nights in the heart of the earth."

In an effort to trick Jesus, the Jewish leaders were always putting him to the test. Many of them had observed our Lord's miracles, but they wanted to see bigger and better things. During the Exodus God parted the Red Sea and sent down manna from heaven. If Jesus were who he claimed to be, he should be able to perform similar miracles. Our Savior was quick to respond to these men, telling them that he did not come to be their miracle worker. Instead, he alluded to his resurrection from the dead, which would prove his divinity to everyone who sought truth.

If we look around us, God's signs are found in both nature and in the lives of people. But how often do we think about the miracles that we live with everyday? If the Lord were to suddenly remove his presence from the world and our personal lives, we would receive an instant lesson on God's miraculous power. All manner of life and creation is a miracle, but countless people never ponder this truth. It is the Holy Spirit who illuminates God's miracles for the searching heart, but our free will allows us to close our eyes. To realize God's transforming presence requires a level of faith that many people do not possess. If we would only slow down and prayerfully examine the wonders of life and the world that we live in. As the saying goes, we need to slow our pace in order to smell the roses. I fear that we have become robots entrenched in technology, moving from one task to another. This lifestyle prevents us from discerning spiritual realities.

The disciples of Jesus were given the ultimate sign of his divinity and power. The empty tomb and their interactions with the risen Christ was the confirmation that carried them through life, providing the strength to proclaim the gospel in the most trying situations. But the risen Jesus is also with us today, speaking to our conscience, hearts, and minds. Our Savior has given us the inner peace that comes through forgiveness, and we have the witness of the Spirit that we are reconciled with God. We, who have been changed by the love and power of God, have received his living Word to internalize. As we apply God's Word to our lives, we become cognizant of past and present miracles, and how the Lord is speaking to us in the present. It all begins with that first step of faith, and the journey continues through increased faith, prayer, and surrender. So many people refuse to step out in faith, thereby closing the door to the Lord's miraculous power in their lives. The signs along our busy highways guide and protect us as we travel from one location to another. But, just as the signs along the road are often ignored, the Lord's spiritual signs receive the same response. God tells us to slow down that we might see and experience his many wonders.

THE PROCLAMATION

Luke 2:8–15

> And there were shepherds living out in the fields nearby, keeping watch over their flocks at night. An angel of the Lord appeared to them, and the glory of the Lord shone around them, and they were terrified. But the angel said to them, "Do not be afraid. I bring you good news of great joy that will be for all people. Today in the town of David a Savior has been born to you; he is Christ the Lord. This will be a sign to you: You will find a baby wrapped in strips of cloth and lying in a manger." Suddenly, a great company of the heavenly host appeared with the angel, praising God and saying, "Glory to God in the highest, and on earth, peace to men on whom his favor rests." When the angels had left them and gone into heaven, the shepherds said to one another, "Let's go to Bethlehem and see this thing that has happened, which the Lord has told us about."

As we examine this reading, an obvious question surfaces. Why would the birth of our Savior be announced to obscure shepherds in a sparsely populated area? One can understand the news eventually reaching them, but to receive this divine proclamation by a host of angels in the night hours seems strange. Why would this historic and life-changing message be proclaimed in such a way? The birth of Jesus could have been announced in Jerusalem, which was the center of Judaism. Or, why not in Bethlehem or other populated areas? Actually, why wasn't it given to the leaders of that day, both Jewish and Roman? Better yet, the angels could have appeared in the heavens with the sound of trumpets, in a manner that everyone would have received the message at one time.

In comparison to the world, the Lord works in and through individuals who would never be considered by society. Moses was an orphan, Rahab lived as a harlot, David was a young shepherd boy, Peter a fisherman, and Matthew a hated tax collector. These are but a few of the biblical figures that God chose to fulfill his will. Rather than looking for influential people of power, the Lord searches for the humble and contrite heart. He seeks those who will be faithful, regardless of the obstacles and trials. Mary, the mother of our Lord, is a prime example of this truth. This is not to say that wealthy and powerful people have not been used for God's glory. Again, it is a matter of the heart and one's willingness to be a servant for a higher purpose.

On that evening many years ago, the Creator of the universe decided that a few humble souls should receive the announcement of our Savior's glorious birth. This speaks to us in many ways, for it affirms our value before God. It tells us that it is our heart that matters, and that the Lord does not favor one person over another. God takes humble individuals and develops them into great servants. Except for Paul, none of the apostles held worldly positions of power. They were common people, who were willing to trust Jesus and commit their life to preaching his message of forgiveness and salvation.

God has not called us because we are great theologians or gifted orators. We are called because of the love of Jesus Christ and his love in our hearts. We are summoned by the Lord to be witnesses of what we have heard and experienced. This requires an open and obedient heart that seeks to follow God's will. Like the shepherds on that dark night many years ago, the Lord continues to call people who will walk in faith and be committed servants.

THE WORD BECAME FLESH

John 1:1, 14

> In the beginning was the Word, and the Word was with God. He was with God in the beginning. The Word became flesh and lived for a while among us. We have seen his glory, the glory of the one and only Son, who came from the Father, full of grace and truth.

The reality of our Savior's birth cannot be denied, for it has changed the hearts of all who have received him in faith. Earthly kingdoms have come and gone, but the kingdom of God, built upon the passion and resurrection of

Jesus Christ, has no end. Students of history have always been interested in tracing great events that have changed the course of time, and the incarnation of Jesus is history's greatest event. All history, past, present, and future, revolves around the birth and life of Jesus. In Christ we see God in human flesh, reaching down to meet us where we are in life. Who can comprehend this mystery? Because it cannot be understood, many people refuse to believe its reality. But how much of creation and life do we understand?

We were not there when the angel Gabriel spoke to Mary, or when the shepherds in the field were told of our Savior's birth. We did not see Jesus in the flesh, or witness his many miracles. When Jesus rose from the dead, we were not with his apostles to see the risen Christ. But through the Holy Spirit we are given the assurance that these events took place. Our proof for the birth of Jesus is found in our spiritual birth. It is seen in the lives of everyone who has internalized the love of Christ. The confirmation for what we have not physically seen is found in the changes that other people see in us. Simply stated, a nonexistent Savior cannot send his living Spirit to transform lives.

The evidence of Jesus' incarnation is also found in the Church, which has stood the test of time with all of its trials. Rather than buildings, the Church is a movement that is empowered by the Holy Spirit. While the Church is imperfect and has struggled with internal sin, the Lord continues to purge it of unrighteousness. Even though the Church reflects a changing society that embraces sin, the faithful will continue to communicate sound doctrine. The Church has always experienced difficulties, but God's truth in Jesus Christ never ceases to change the lives of those who respond in faith.

The birth of Jesus is the link between God and our eternal destiny. When Mary was told that her son would save the people from their sins, she could not imagine the path that Jesus would take, nor was she aware of her role in God's plans for the world. Instead, she simply agreed to be the Lord's servant, allowing God to use her life according to his providence. Her faith was manifested before Jesus was born, and it never wavered. She trusted the Lord, knowing that her life would be in his care and used for a glorious purpose.

In spite of global violence, the Spirit of the risen Christ is everywhere, convicting people of their sins and trying to move them toward peace and reconciliation with God. The birth of Jesus is not merely a historical event, but rather God entering our world to save us from ourselves. Jesus was born into the world that we might be changed and live in hope.

Sixteen

THANKFULNESS

THANKFUL HEARTS

Psalm 89:1; 100:4; 136:2, 3

> I will sing of the Lord forever. With my mouth I will make your faithfulness known through all generations. I will declare that your love stands firm.
> Enter his gates with thanksgiving and his courts with praise. Give thanks to him, and praise his name. For the Lord is good, and his love endures forever.
> Give thanks to the God of gods. His love endures forever. Give thanks to the Lord of lords. His love endures forever.

It is the thankful heart that is close to God, receiving the fullness of his grace. But countless people, including professing Christians, live each day without the thought of praising the Lord for his endless gifts. How can they fail to see the Lord's mercy and sustaining presence in their lives? The sinful nature fools us into believing that our gifts and power are created by us. People believe that their achievements result from their own knowledge and wisdom. What a sad commentary for a world that is totally dependent upon its Creator for everything, including the air that we breathe.

God's grace is poured out upon everyone, both the righteous and the unrighteous. His gifts are given that they might be used to his glory. It is the Lord's perfect knowledge and compassion that makes his presence known, and it is this presence that sustains us through life's trials. But in spite of this reality, we allow ourselves to be deceived by thinking that we have created our gifts and opportunities. Christians know that apart from the Lord's infinite love and abiding grace, we would live in a joyless and hopeless void.

Sometimes our spiritual lives can better be understood by using human analogies. For example, no one would argue that our young children are totally dependent upon us for everything. However, isn't it true that on occasion their attitudes and behavior communicate something different? In other words, our children tend to believe that they are adult enough to make their own decisions and support themselves. When these attitudes prevail, they are certainly not thankful for what we do for them, including our sacrifices and the pain that we often endure.

We know the feeling when our children go through life failing to acknowledge our love and assistance. Parents experience pain when their children never say thank you. Depending upon the situation, they may even experience frustration and anger. Now, if we use this analogy in a spiritual sense, it is easy to understand how the Lord feels when we live as ungrateful children. God's gifts are endless, and the sacrifice of his Son for our salvation is beyond comprehension.

We are clay in the Potter's hands, meaning that the Lord is our Creator, and it is his sovereignty and providence that we are to accept in faith. We came into this world naked, and we will leave it in the same manner. The question is, what will our hearts reflect when we depart this life? Will they be hearts of thanksgiving and praise? The Psalms are full of praise and thanksgiving to God, and these heart offerings continued throughout the early Church. The apostle Paul wrote that we should give thanks to God at all times and in all places, for it is through continuous praise and thanksgiving that we deepen our relationship with our Creator.

REJOICE IN THE LORD

Philippians 4:4–7

> Rejoice in the Lord always. I will say it again:
> Rejoice! Let your gentleness be evident to all. The Lord is near. Do not be anxious about anything, but in everything, by prayer and petition, with thanksgiving, present your requests to God. And the peace of God, which transcends all understanding, will guard your hearts and your minds in Christ Jesus.

Philippi was a Roman colony and a strong military outpost when this letter was written. Paul laid the groundwork for the first church in Philippi during his second missionary journey, and he maintained contact with the people. It is believed that Paul was imprisoned in Rome awaiting trial when this epistle was sent. Although the Philippian church seems to have been the least troublesome of all the churches, Paul felt the need to address certain issues, including those of a relational nature.

Paul was experiencing God's joy while he was imprisoned, even though his execution was evident. Rather than seeing himself as a victim, he rejoiced that he could suffer for Jesus Christ and the gospel. He understood his situation as a means through which God would be glorified. Paul knew that he would experience perfect joy in the next life, but his present life in the Spirit enabled him to have peace and joy in all circumstances. His focus was on the Lord, and how he could be a witness to God's love and power.

Paul was convinced that God is present in all of our trials, providing the strength that is needed. He was also cognizant that one's misfortunes can provide opportunities to communicate the message and promises of Christ. His imprisonment afforded some unique and powerful ways to accomplish this. In defending himself against the government's accusations, he would have the chance to share the gospel with influential Roman officials. Paul was an educated Roman citizen; therefore, his case drew attention, and this in itself was a channel for the gospel. Additionally, Paul's faith and firm stand was a witness to other Christians, giving them renewed strength and hope. Even today, he continues to be a witness for Christians who are enduring difficult times.

Adversity will come to all Christians, for we live in an imperfect and sinful world. The question is not whether trials will come, but rather how we will face them. Will we see them as a means for personal growth and an opportunity to share the gospel? Our joy is lost when we perceive ourselves as victims, rather than people of faith and power. Paul reveals that we should rejoice that we are one with our Savior, sharing in the divine suffering that brought the gospel of reconciliation to the world.

The Philippian church was founded while Paul and Silas were imprisoned in Philippi for preaching the gospel. While incarcerated, their joy and witness led to the conversion of the Philippian jailer and his family. What a message for us today! When we surrender our lives to God, he will use all of our situations to his glory. Joy is a gift of the Spirit that comes to those who give their heart and soul to the Lord. Paul knew that joy was not dependent upon circumstances, but rather the life we live in Christ. To have Jesus Christ in our heart is to possess his peace and joy.

ONLY ONE GAVE THANKS

Luke 17:11–19

> On his way to Jerusalem, Jesus traveled along the border between Samaria and Galilee. As he was going into a village, ten men who had leprosy met him. They

stood at a distance and called out to him in a loud voice, "Jesus, Master, have pity on us." When he saw them, he said, "Go, show yourselves to the priests." And as they went, they were cleansed. One of them, when he saw he was healed, came back, praising God in a loud voice. He threw himself at Jesus' feet and thanked him—and he was a Samaritan. Jesus asked, "Were not all ten men cleansed? Where are the other nine? Was no one found to return and give praise to God except this foreigner?" Then he said to him, "Rise and go; your faith has made you well."

On his way to Jerusalem, somewhere between Samaria and Galilee, ten lepers approached Jesus. We are told that they were standing at the entrance to the city. It seems obvious that they had heard of Jesus, for they cried out to him to have pity on them. The Jews believed that leprosy was a punishment from God for sin; therefore, those who were afflicted with the disease were sent to priests rather than doctors. In this case, the priests would decide whether they were healed and could return to the population. The law compelled lepers to keep their distance from people, and it appears that they did.

The lepers' request was an act of faith, for it is apparent that they thought Jesus could do something for them. Our Savior responded, but he did not engage in conversation. He simply told them to go to the priests for the certification of their healings. By doing this, Jesus was putting their faith to the test. The text suggests that when they started out, they still had the disease and were healed en route. Can you imagine the joy that took place when all ten lepers were transformed and set free from their pain and hopeless state. The sad commentary to this story is that only one of these individuals returned to Jesus to give thanks and to praise the Lord for the healing. It seems that when people fail to thank God immediately, they don't thank him at all, and this was the situation here. The surprise for anyone hearing this story is that only the foreigner was thankful. It was the one lacking spiritual privileges who returned to give thanks.

This story certainly speaks to faith, but the focus is upon one's response to God's grace. The Lord's love touches us everyday, but few people respond with praise and thanksgiving. We often forget that God's gifts and miracles are continuous. While the nine lepers manifested faith in the Savior and were unquestionably joyful over their complete healing, they lacked a thankful heart. For Christians, being thankful takes in every aspect of life. It is not simply thanking the Lord for certain things, but rather for all gifts, both large and small. When people have thankful hearts they see God's presence and grace in all aspects of life.

As we look at the life and ministry of Jesus, we find that he continuously gave thanks. Even though he is the Son of God, he always gave the Father praise. He thanked the Father for his disciples, for his sustenance, and for the miracles that were performed. In Revelation, the apostle John wrote that all glory, wisdom, and thanksgiving belong to our God. Apart from God's mercy, we would exist in a world void of love and hope. Who among us can live apart from the Lord's gifts, including the grace that sustains us? The question is, do we realize these gifts, and are we offering up our praise?

SING A NEW SONG

Psalm 98

> Sing to the Lord a new song, for he has done marvelous things; his right hand and his holy arm have worked salvation for him. The Lord has made his salvation known, and revealed his righteousness to the nations. He has remembered his love and his faithfulness to the house of Israel; all the ends of the earth have seen the salvation of our God. Shout for joy to the Lord, all the earth, burst into jubilant song with music; make music to the Lord with the harp, with the harp and the sound of singing, with trumpets and the blast of the ram's horn— shout for joy before the Lord, the King. Let the sea resound, and all that is in it. Let the rivers clap their hands, let them sing together for joy, let them sing before the Lord, for he comes to judge the earth. He will judge the world in righteousness, and the peoples with equity.

This psalm, written by an unknown author, exhorts Israel to offer up a new song to the Lord. It focuses upon the marvelous things that God has done for them, including their historical deliverance from Egyptian bondage. Regardless of Israel's sins, the Lord was always faithful to them, making his salvation known and revealing his righteousness to the nation. According to the psalmist, the earth continuously experiences God's power and salvation. In a psalm of thanks to the Lord, King David wrote, "Sing to the Lord all the earth, proclaim his salvation day after day. Declare his glory among the nations, his marvelous deeds among all peoples. For great is the Lord and most worthy of praise."

Who can fathom the wonders and power of the Lord? It is God who created and sustains the universe and all life. He is the artist of the seasons, the fountain for the mighty waters, and the gravity that keeps the galaxies in place. The world has been given a divine order that sustains life. Our Creator's power and beauty are found everywhere, but we need spiritual eyes to realize it. Without spiritual sensitivity we are blind to God's creating and sustaining presence. The psalmist wrote, "Let the sea resound, and all that is in it. Let the rivers clap their hands, let them sing together for joy, let them sing before the Lord."

This psalm also praises God for the perfect justice that is promised believers. Justice in this world is imperfect and often corrupt, but when Jesus returns he will administer divine justice. We read that "God will judge the world in righteousness, and the peoples with equity." During times of trial we must trust in the Lord's promise of justice and equality. Those who now struggle under the weight of humanity's sins will receive God's perfect and eternal justice.

In addition to the Lord's marvelous deeds, creative power, and promise of justice, is the salvation that has been made known to us. The psalmist praised God, saying, "His right hand and his holy arm have worked salvation for him. The Lord has made his salvation known, and revealed his righteousness to the nations." As seen with the life of Abraham, the way of salvation has always been through God's grace and our faith, but through the sacrificial life and death of Jesus Christ we now have an intercessor and advocate, who completely identifies with our humanity and trials. Let us give praise and thanks for the saving grace that flows through Christ.

GIVING THANKS IN ALL CIRCUMSTANCES

I Thessalonians 5:12–18

> Now we ask you brothers to respect those who work hard among you, who are over you in the Lord, and who admonish you. Hold them in the highest regard in love because of their work. Live in peace with each other. And we urge you brothers, warn those who are idle, encourage the timid, help the weak, be patient with everyone. Make sure that nobody pays back wrong for wrong, but always try to be kind to each other and to everyone else. Be joyful always, pray continually, give thanks in all circumstances, for this is God's will for you in Christ Jesus.

There are many lessons in this passage, but our focus is upon Paul's words relating to giving thanks. Without thankful hearts, we are unable to serve God and one another. It is important, therefore, that we see God's presence in all that we do, realizing that he is our strength and guide through life. Thanksgiving is not simply a word or a yearly holiday to celebrate with family and friends. Instead, it is a life that recognizes the Lord as our Shepherd and source of present and eternal hope. Rather than irregular responses of praise and thanksgiving, Christians are to thank the Lord in every situation. Although this is difficult during times of trial, it is the spiritual channel for increased faith and grace. When Paul wrote the Thessalonians that they were to give thanks in all circumstances, he knew that such expressions are the continuing source for personal renewal and inner strength.

Giving thanks is the heart praising God for needs being met. It is also an acknowledgment that only God can satisfy the hunger of the soul and bring meaning to life. There is a song that is often sung by children, which reads, "Count your blessings, count them one by one." Have you ever taken the time to think about all the blessings you have received from God on a daily basis? We often forget that the air we breathe is a blessing, as well as the gifts of family and friends. The greatest gift from God is Jesus Christ, through whom we have forgiveness and salvation. All of our blessings are gifts of divine grace that we so often take for granted. In fact, what we give to others are simply those things that God has already given to us. No blessing originates with us, whether material or spiritual.

The beginning of wisdom comes when we realize our total dependence upon the Lord. As the psalmist wrote, "Praise God from whom all blessings flow." We lose our intimacy with God and our opportunity for spiritual growth when we fail to realize this. The sad truth is that few people praise God for the daily blessings in their life, let alone the gifts that stand out. What is astonishing is that there are those who find nothing for which to give thanks. Rather than praising God for what they have, they complain about what they believe they should have. Paul exhorted his fellow Christians to give thanks for everything, at all times and in all places, for this is God's will. We do this because God is always with us, offering his grace in all situations.

People often become hurt and upset when they are not thanked when doing things for others. This is especially true with our children, who continuously receive our gifts. Our heavenly Father never ceases to give to his children, but few of them offer up thankful hearts. May each of us open our hearts to the countless blessings bestowed upon us by our merciful Creator.

Seventeen

WITNESS FOR GOD

A GLOWING WITNESS

Exodus 34:29–35

> When Moses came down from Mount Sinai with the two tablets of the Testimony in his hands, he was not aware that his face was radiant because he had spoken with the Lord. When Aaron and all the Israelites saw Moses, his face was radiant, and they were afraid to come near him. But Moses called to them, so Aaron and all the leaders of the community came back to him, and he spoke to them. Afterward, all the Israelites came near him, and he gave them all the commands the Lord had given him on Mount Sinai. When Moses finished speaking to them, he put a veil over his face. But whenever he entered the Lord's presence to speak with him, he removed the veil until he came out. And when he came out and told the Israelites what he had been commanded, they saw that his face was radiant. Then Moses would put the veil back over his face until he went in to speak to the Lord.

When Moses came down from Mount Sinai he was unaware that his face was glowing. The Hebrew literally reads that his face sent out rays. Moses was a witness of God's awesome power and glory, and it was communicated to the Israelites. The appearance of Moses frightened Aaron and the people, causing them to flee from him. Can you imagine someone glowing in your presence? You might think that it was the result of the nuclear radiation that we all fear.

Moses had been in the presence of the Almighty, and it was not long before the people realized that this was the reason for his radiance. He prayed that

God would reveal his glory, and his prayers were answered. Moses not only saw the Lord's glory, but he also received it. There would be no mistake among the people that he was anointed to be their leader. He had been in God's presence for forty days of unbroken fellowship, and his spirit and appearance reflected this. I learned from a jeweler that some diamonds, after being exposed to the light, retain their brightness and emit light in a dark environment. Like a diamond exposed to God's all-consuming presence, Moses emitted light in a world darkened by sin. It appears that Moses was initially unaware of his glowing face. This is the way it is with Christians, whose humility blinds them to their own radiance. No artist can paint God's glory, nor can it be created by an earthly power. It results from a surrendered heart that is filled with divine love.

With a career in law enforcement, I interviewed many witnesses who claimed to have experienced something, but their stories often left room for doubt. But when we experience Jesus Christ the facts are clear. The human heart changes, and we are aware of it. We may not literally glow, but we communicate a glowing persona that others are able to sense. When Christ is in our hearts we become new people, who are filled with sensitivity, love, and compassion. Our perceptions and philosophy of life begin to mirror that of our Savior. This is the glow that others see when they interact with us. It is the Spirit's glow within us, communicating to others. Through Moses the people saw the glory of God and the light of truth, and this speaks to us. What do people see and experience through our lives? Does the life of Christ shine forth from us?

CHRISTIAN LAMPS

Luke 11:33–36

> No one lights a lamp and puts it in a place where it will be hidden, or under a bowl. Instead, he puts it on its stand, so that those who come in may see the light. Your eye is the lamp of your body. When your eyes are good, your whole body also is full of light. But when they are bad, your body also is full of darkness. See to it, then, that the light within you is not darkness. Therefore, if your whole body is full of light, and no part of it dark, it will be completely lighted, as when the light of a lamp shines on you.

To understand this lesson, we must examine some key words, the first of which is our Lord's figurative use of the human eye. Jesus said, "Your eye is the lamp of your body." The employment of this word seems strange, but the meaning is clear. Jesus is telling us that our sight, how we perceive life, determines the amount of light within us. He is alluding to spiritual vision and light. In other words, do we see spiritual truth, and are we allowing that truth to take root in our life? Obviously, the more truth we allow into our lives, the better witnesses we become for God.

The light that Jesus speaks about is the indwelling presence of the Holy Spirit, who fills our life with God's glory. It is the light of God shining forth in a world darkened by sin. I am reminded of King Saul, who was a great leader of the Israelites. He was filled with the light of God's anointing and a spiritual example for the people. But Saul's vision became blurred and began to deteriorate. Saul thought he could do things his way, to the exclusion of the Lord. He found out, however, that poor vision leads to sin and the loss of divine power. Jesus said that when your eyes are bad you become full of darkness. The light of the Holy Spirit left Saul, just as it leaves so many people who believe that they can make decisions and live without God. Poor vision leads to disobedience, with the result being darkness. Can you imagine trying to live without natural light? A soul that lives in spiritual darkness is lost in a world of sin.

Jesus also speaks about the purpose of a lamp, stating that no one lights a lamp and then puts it in a place where the light is obscured. We, of course, are the lamps that our Savior is speaking about. Like the lamps in our homes, they may be beautiful on the outside, but they must serve a purpose. Christian lamps shine with divine wattage, and wherever they are there is a beautiful glow for everyone to see. It is a glow that comes from a heart that is filled with the love of Jesus Christ.

Everything begins with our vision, whether we possess the sight to see spiritual realities. Those who internalize God's truth and love emit the light of the Holy Spirit, and they become Christian lamps that reveal Jesus Christ to the world. Everyone must check their vision to determine how well they see. Do we see the need for God in every area of our life? If so, have we reached out in faith and received the gifts and glowing power of the Holy Spirit? And finally, what kind of lamps are we? Do we project an intermittent and flickering light, or are we a floodlight for Christ? To prevent falling into darkness, it is important that we continuously examine our spiritual vision.

A CALL TO SEPARATION

II Corinthians 6:14–18; 7:1

> Do not be yoked together with unbelievers. For what do righteousness and wickedness have in common? Or what fellowship can light have with darkness? What harmony is there between Christ and Belial? What does a believer have

in common with an unbeliever? What agreement is there between the temple of God and idols? For we are the temple of the living God. As God has said: "I will live with them and walk among them, and I will be their God, and they will be my people. Therefore come out from them and be separate, says the Lord. Touch no unclean thing, and I will receive you. I will be a Father to you, and you will be my sons and daughters," says the Lord Almighty. Since we have these promises, dear friends, let us purify ourselves from everything that contaminates body and spirit, perfecting holiness out of reverence for God.

Christians are to be in the world, yet spiritually separate from it. Although we are sent to be witnesses in the darkest corners of life, we must separate ourselves from sin. As the salt of the earth the Lord wants us to be everywhere, but we must always stand firm upon God's Word. Jesus left his throne of glory to be a guiding light for sinners, and as his body we are to do the same. We are separate in the sense that we are set apart for God's purposes. Jesus ate and drank with sinners, but he was not part of their sinful world. He was totally separated unto the Father, which enabled people to know the presence of God. As a beacon of light, he was an example for all to see. Jesus told the people that to see him was to see the Father, for he and the Father are one.

When the sinful world looked at Jesus, they saw the holiness and perfect love of God. In Christ they experienced the beauty of life in human flesh, and this spoke to their own potential. Although Jesus lived amongst sinners, he was far from them. This is the life that we are to live, one that reveals the glory of the Lord to those lost in sin. This is accomplished when we are in the world but spiritually separated from it, living the example of Jesus. In his communion with the Father, Jesus said, "My prayer is not that you take them out of the world, but that you protect them from the evil one. They are not of the world, even as I am not of it. Sanctify them by the truth; your Word is truth. As you have sent me into the world, I have sent them into the world. For them I sanctify myself, that they too may truly be sanctified."

Although we may seldom give thought to how our lives impact upon others, everything we say and do has its influences. The positive example that we communicate is directly related to our love and maturity in the Spirit. To be separated unto God means standing up for righteousness and what is just for all people. Compromise with any manner of sin is not the sanctified life. While there are only two roads one can travel, many people try to walk both paths at the same time. The apostle Paul wrote that we must purify ourselves from everything that defiles both body and spirit, walking in holiness out of reverence for God. This is the sanctified life of the Christian.

THE MODEL CHURCH

I Thessalonians 1:2–10

> We always thank God for all of you, mentioning you in our prayers. We continually remember before our God and Father your work produced by faith, your labor prompted by love, and your endurance inspired by hope in our Lord Jesus Christ. Brothers loved by God, we know that he has chosen you, because our gospel came to you, not simply with words, but also with power, with the Holy Spirit and with deep conviction. You know how we lived among you for your sake. You became imitators of us and of the Lord; in spite of severe suffering, you welcomed the message with joy given by the Holy Spirit. And so, you became a model to all the believers in Macedonia and Achaia—your faith in God has become known everywhere. Therefore, we do not need to say anything about it, for they themselves report what kind of reception you gave us. They tell how you turned from idols to serve the living and true God, and to wait for his Son from heaven, whom he raised from the dead—Jesus, who rescues us from the coming wrath.

This letter was sent to the church in Thessalonica, which was a city and seaport in Macedonia, a province in Greece. The city was located on the Egyptian Way, which was a heavily traveled route. Paul, Silas, and Timothy went to Thessalonica on their second missionary trip. It was the second place that the gospel was preached in Europe. Philippi, which is also in Greece, was the first city to hear the good news of Jesus Christ.

The beauty of the Thessalonian church was not found in large cathedrals or beautiful buildings, but rather in the people. They were examples of love, faith, and endurance that result from surrendering one's life to Jesus Christ. The apostle Paul was noted for praising God when believers remained committed to Christ, and in this letter we find glowing words. He wrote, "We always thank God for all of you, mentioning you in our prayers." It was a joy for Paul and his companions to see the church filled with the Holy Spirit and growing in understanding and faith. The ministry of Paul and his coworkers led the Thessalonians out of idol worship and into the saving grace of Jesus, and they were joyful at their spiritual growth.

There is a tendency to think of the Church as a building, which is often punctuated by the amount of time and money that is put into church structures. Pastors know the emphasis that is placed on buildings, often to the exclusion of the ministry. I have participated in many meetings in which the church building and financial investments took precedence over everything. If it were not for the building and related issues, there would be nothing to talk about at some monthly church meetings. It is usually up to the pastor or other concerned leaders to bring up topics of worship and ministry.

The Thessalonians were not burdened with building maintenance and the cost of church additions. Their total focus was upon their new life in Christ, and how they could serve God and reach out to others. This is what Paul commended them for, and the reason why he gave praise to God. In spite of their afflictions and an uncertain future, their joy came from within. It was a peace and contentment that resulted from a changed heart and renewed hope. Through the Holy Spirit they knew that they were forgiven and reconciled with God. As Paul stated, they were rescued from the wrath to come. They were a model for all believers, and their example continues today through this inspired writing. May their faith, love, and endurance serve to inspire and motivate us.

LISTENING AND DOING

James 1:19–26

> My dear brothers, take note of this: Everyone should be quick to listen, slow to speak, and slow to become angry, for man's anger does not bring about the righteous life that God desires. Therefore, get rid of all moral filth and the evil that is so prevalent, and humbly accept the word planted in you, which can save you. Do not merely listen to the word and so deceive yourselves. Do what it says. Anyone who listens to the word but does not do what it says is like a man who looks at his face in the mirror and, after looking at himself, goes away and immediately forgets what he looks like. But the man who looks intently into the perfect law that gives freedom and continues to do this, not forgetting what he has heard, but doing it—he will be blessed in what he does. Anyone who considers himself religious and yet, does not keep a tight rein on his tongue, he deceives himself and his religion is worthless.

The apostle James wrote this letter to the twelve tribes, which were scattered among the nations. It was a general epistle that was meant for all Christians. In this writing he addresses the importance of listening to God's Word and living in its light. He tells us that we must be quick to listen and slow to speak, practicing humility through self-examination and acceptance of the Lord's teachings.

We live in a world of superficial words, meaningless conversations, and empty expressions. There are also deceptions that we must continuously filter out of our interactions. It seems that everyone wants to be heard, but few people have the desire to listen to others. This carries over into our spiritual lives, especially when it comes to listening to God's Word and applying it to our lives. Rather than support and encourage others, our words often destroy relationships. This is why James implores us to be quick to listen and slow to speak. During my years of counseling individuals and couples, I have learned how hurting words negatively impact upon a person's life, sometimes damaging their self-esteem. This, of course, may lead to other personal issues in one's life.

James wrote that, although the tongue is a small part of the body, it makes great boasts and is capable of setting the world on fire. This truth is clearly seen with politicians, whose threatening words lead their countries into wars. Paul wrote the Thessalonians that they should live a quiet life, tending to their own business. If everyone were to do this there would be little conflict between people and countries. Careful listeners allow time to weigh what they have heard. They are also able to hear the quiet voice of God speaking to their heart and conscience.

Those who listen and digest the Lord's teachings are able to live the Christian life, for they see themselves and their relationships within the context of God's will. True listening also brings the reflection that results in emotional and spiritual development. Many people believe that they are listening, but the process is incomplete if the lessons are not applied to one's life. The truths that we hear are often thought to be for others, rather than for ourselves. Let us prayerfully heed the apostle's words by becoming listeners and doers of God's Word.

Eighteen

DISOBEDIENCE AND THE END TIMES

JONAH'S RELATIONSHIPS

Jonah 1:1–7

> The word of the Lord came to Jonah son of Amittai: "Go to the great city of Nineveh and preach against it, because its wickedness has come up before me." But Jonah ran away from the Lord and headed for Tarshish. He went down to Joppa, where he found a ship bound for that port. After paying the fare, he went aboard and sailed for Tarshish to flee from the Lord. Then the Lord sent a great wind on the sea, and such a violent storm arose that the ship threatened to break up. All the sailors were afraid and each cried out to his own god. And they threw the cargo into the sea to lighten the ship. But Jonah had gone below deck, where he lay down and fell into a deep sleep. The captain went to him and said, "How can you sleep? Get up and call on your god! Maybe he will take notice of us, and we will not perish." The sailors said to each other, "Come, let us cast lots to find out who is responsible for this calamity." They cast lots, and the lot fell on Jonah.

As I read this story, two things stood out in my mind. The first was the beauty of the seaside city of Joppa. Years ago I visited the port where Jonah boarded the ship for Tarshish. While at that location I recalled the story of how his disobedience brought him to the port. I also thought about the violent storm that Jonah experienced and the reaction of the sailors, insisting that everyone pray to their god. It brought back memories of my navy days, when I served aboard an aircraft carrier. On a Mediterranean cruise our ship was caught in a severe hurricane, and I clearly remember the anxiety and fear of the deck crew. I am sure that many sailors were praying to God on that day.

The events relating to this text were quite dramatic, for the ship was in danger of sinking, and the crew was desperately trying to find the cause for what was occurring. They believed that one of the gods was angry at someone on board the ship, and each person was asked to pray to their god. The sailors then had everyone cast lots to determine the guilty one, and the lot fell on Jonah. One can imagine the shock when Jonah was seen as the guilty party. But as we know, Jonah was not right with God. He disobeyed the Lord by refusing to preach to the people of Nineveh, and now he was in trouble with the ship's crew.

Jonah was a prophet who claimed to be a righteous man, but he had no intention of traveling five hundred miles to the Assyrian city of Nineveh. The Lord was sending him to warn the people that unless they repented, there would be a divine judgment. Although Jonah knew that his mission could save the lives of thousands of people, he was obstinate and filled with pride. He only cared about himself and how the trip would be too much of a sacrifice, especially for people that he did not care about. But trying to flee from God was a mistake, and it wasn't long before he realized it. He learned that you cannot hide from the Lord and the responsibilities that he gives you. God sent a storm to apprehend him, and we know the rest of the story.

When we disobey and try to run away from God, we are confronted with storms that stop us in our tracks. They are storms that begin within our hearts, affecting our relationship with God and others. Like Jonah's uncaring heart, the destructive actions of people will always be discovered and brought before the Lord. When we disobey God we lose the blessings that he intends for us.

A SAD FUNERAL

Ecclesiastes 8:8–10

> No man has power over the wind to contain it; so no one has power over the day of his death. As no one is discharged in time of war, so wickedness will not release those who practice it. All this I saw, as I applied my mind to everything done under the sun. There is a time when a man lords it over others to his own hurt. Then too, I saw the wicked buried—those who used to come and go from the holy place and receive praise in the city where they did this. This too is meaningless.

Ecclesiastes was written by King Solomon, primarily to show the vanity of life when we choose to reject God. According to Solomon, you may have the world's riches and be surrounded with praise, but without God there is spiritual poverty and inner emptiness. It's all vanity! Searching for true happiness and fulfillment apart from the Lord is like trying to capture the wind. The impact of this truth is realized at the time of death.

Funerals can bring feelings of sadness, inner loneliness, and despair, as well as guilt and anger. But someone's death may also produce self-examination with the living. One may even ponder questions relating to the purpose of life. Having officiated at many funerals, I am aware of the range of emotions felt by those in attendance, including the anger directed toward God. Whether the deceased is a king or pauper, funerals are a solemn time when we pause to think about many things, including life's deepest mysteries, especially those relating to the spiritual world and our relationship with God.

As he watched the wicked being buried, Solomon thought about their life, how they would attend the temple and receive praise from people. Knowing that they were sinful people, he now contemplated their death. The praise that they received when they were alive was pointless, for it would not follow them into eternity. Regardless of how wicked people are, there is a tendency to make them saints when they die. It is as though death somehow transforms them into another person. We all know, however, that this is not reality. When unrepentant sinners die they are left outside the kingdom, awaiting God's final judgment.

What makes a funeral sad is the lost state of those who die in their sins. No clergy person or ritual can bring the wicked into God's eternal realm. Countless people, who are affiliated with the Church, will never see the kingdom of God. Jesus continuously spoke about this in his teachings, warning his listeners that death seals one's destiny, terminating any opportunity for a change of heart.

Solomon knew that ritualistic obedience, knowledge of the law, and works were no assurance of salvation. What a message for people today, who believe that these things make them spiritual and worthy of God's kingdom. Such individuals are ignoring the voice of the Spirit, who is convicting them of their sins and leading them to Jesus Christ. Pride and self-will keep so many people from God's grace! At the time of death, everyone's mask will be removed, revealing who they really are. Let us now, while there is time, make the changes that result in a pure heart.

THE NARROW DOOR

Luke 13:22–30

> Then Jesus went through the towns and villages, teaching as he made his way to Jerusalem. Someone asked him, "Lord, are only a few people going to be

saved?" He said to them, "Make every effort to enter through the narrow door, because many, I tell you, will try to enter and will not be able to. Once the owner of the house gets up and closes the door, you will stand outside knocking and pleading, 'Sir, open the door for us.' But he will answer, 'I don't know you or where you come from.' Then you will say, 'We ate and drank with you, and you taught us in our streets.' But he will reply, 'I don't know you or where you come from. Away from me, all you evildoers!' There will be weeping there, and gnashing of teeth, when you see Abraham, Isaac and Jacob and all the prophets in the kingdom of God, but you yourselves thrown out. People will come from east and west and north and south, and will take their places at the feast in the kingdom of God. Indeed there are those who are last who will be first, and first who will be last."

Luke reports someone asking Jesus about the kingdom of God, wanting to know if just a small number of people were going to be saved. If you noted, Jesus did not respond with a yes or no answer. Instead, he told a story that would make his listeners examine their lives. The question was relevant because there were different beliefs about God's kingdom, even amongst the religious leaders of that time. But Jesus was not concerned about theology and statistics. Rather than place a number on how many people will find salvation, his answer showed concern for individual souls. He said, "make every effort to enter through the narrow gate." The word *effort* in this sentence can be translated as *agonizing*. In other words, Jesus emphasized that we must be agonizing in our effort. The questioner came seeking statistics, and he was suddenly confronted with his own spirituality.

Jesus forced this inquisitive individual to look at his own life, and we must do the same. Are we making an agonizing effort to enter through the narrow door? Jesus informs us that many people will claim to have known him, but they will not be saved. He makes it clear that we need a personal relationship with him, not simply knowledge and affiliation. Either we have given our lives to Jesus in faith, or we have not. Many people are in some way connected with the Church and may even be in leadership and teaching positions, but it does not mean that they are walking in the teachings of Christ.

Jesus reveals the frustration and anger that will take place when the door to God's kingdom is closed, leaving people outside begging for entrance. They will say, "Sir, open the door for us." But he will answer, "I don't know you or where you come from." They will then tell Jesus that they interacted with him and heard his teachings in the streets. This is a tragic picture of individuals who have a certain proximity to Jesus, but they never gave their lives to him. As such, our Savior does not have a personal relationship with them.

The end of this lesson graphically shows the finality of those who cast aside the opportunities to personally know Jesus Christ. Realizing their eternal separation from God, their frustration turns into anger and despair. Jesus informs us that there will be weeping and gnashing of teeth when the unsaved see others enter God's kingdom, with the door closing behind them. This, however, is not the Lord's will, for his love reaches out to everyone. God gave us his greatest gift, the life and sacrificial death of his Son. Through the life of Christ everyone is offered saving grace. The tragedy is that people willfully reject God's love, thereby bringing judgment upon themselves.

THE REALITY AND WORKS OF SATAN

Ephesians 6:10–18

> Be strong in the Lord and in his mighty power. Put on the full armor of God so that you can take your stand against the devil's schemes. For our struggle is not against flesh and blood, but against the rulers, against the authorities, against the powers of this dark world and against the spiritual forces of evil in the heavenly realms. Therefore put on the full armor of God, so that when the day of evil comes, you may be able to stand your ground, and after you have done everything, to stand. Stand firm then, with the belt of truth buckled around your waist, with the breastplate of righteousness in place, and with your feet fitted with the readiness that comes from the gospel of peace. In addition to all of this, take up the shield of faith, with which you can extinguish all the flaming arrows of the evil one. Take the helmet of salvation and the sword of the Spirit, which is the word of God. And pray in the Spirit on all occasions with all kinds of prayers and requests. With this in mind, be alert and keep on praying for all the saints.

Paul wanted the Christians in Ephesus to know that they were in a spiritual battle between good and evil. As such, they needed the full armor of God to protect them from the works of the devil. The analogy and imagery used by Paul to communicate his message reflected the battle dress of the Roman soldier. Paul knew how important each piece was for the soldier's protection, and how a missing piece of armor could result in death. While imprisoned, Paul saw soldiers putting on their battle gear, and this led him to make this spiritual analogy.

The existence of Satan is taught in seven books of the Hebrew Bible and by every New Testament writer, including our Savior's teachings. The Scriptures paint a clear picture of Satan's personality and nature, how he fell from grace, taking with him a third of the angelic force. The Bible speaks about Satan's intentions, which are revealed in his ongoing works of evil. The Lord's inspired writers have many names for him, all of which manifest his deceptiveness. Jesus calls him the devil, which means slanderer. Matthew refers to Satan as Beelzebub or lord of dirt. The apostle John calls him the evil one, prince of this world, accuser of the brethren, the serpent or dragon, murderer, liar, and a confirmed sinner. Paul describes him as the tempter, god of this age, prince of the power of the air, and the angel of light. Peter simply gave him the title of adversary, which sums it all up. Satan was the first sinner, and Paul tells us that his sin was pride. He wanted to exalt himself above God and to possess and rule the world.

Since his fall from grace, Satan has not stood still in his mission to spread evil. He is determined to destroy as many souls as possible. Like an arsonist who starts a fire and becomes excited at the disastrous results, Satan has given birth to the sinful nature. John Wesley said that the devil's first work is to destroy the kingdom of God within us. Satan's key weapon is planting doubt in the hearts and minds of people, a method that proved successful in the Garden of Eden. He mingles truth with falsehood, in an effort to appear godly and concerned about our welfare. As the angel of light, Satan strives to make things look good and right. In some instances he even convinces people that he does not exist, that evil is simply an illusion. Many Christians have been snared in this trap, and the numbers seem to be growing. If Satan does not exist, there is no need for a Savior, and this is the final blow for those who have fallen prey to godlessness.

As Paul states, our struggle is not against flesh and blood, but rather against the rulers, powers, and forces of darkness. Satan has planted the seeds of sin, including those of pride, deception, self-will, and doubt. He has also planted the seeds of discouragement, diversion, and spiritual apathy. The Bible warns us about Satan's existence and his mission, emphasizing that there is a war raging over our souls. This is why we need the full armor of God, which is a life that is completely surrendered to the Lord.

Like a soldier, we must wear our battle dress everyday and be ready for spiritual warfare. No part of our lives is to be vulnerable to Satan's attacks. In the wilderness Jesus was tempted by the devil for forty days and nights. When Satan finally left him, we are told that it was only until an opportune time. If the Son of God was relentlessly attacked by the devil, what does this say to us? There is no level of spiritual maturity that removes us from the influences and power of evil. This is the great battlefield, where the army of God fights the adversary day and night.

The question is not whether evil exists, for it is all around us. Our concern speaks to the spiritual strength necessary to fight the many faces of evil in the world. Are we truly wearing the full armor of God? Does our battle dress include the belt of truth, the breastplate of righteousness, and the readiness that comes from the gospel of peace? Have we taken up the shield of faith, and are we wearing the helmet of salvation? Do we stand firm upon God's Word, and is our life committed to prayer?

BASEMENT BARGAINING

Matthew 19:16–22

> Now a man came up to Jesus and asked, "Teacher, what good thing must I do to get eternal life?" "Why do you ask me about what is good?" Jesus replied. "There is only One who is good. If you want to enter life, obey the commandments." "Which ones?" the man inquired. Jesus replied, "Do not murder, do not commit adultery, do not steal, do not give false testimony, honor your father and mother, and love your neighbor as yourself." "All these I have kept," the young man said. "What do I still lack?" Jesus answered, "If you want to be perfect, go sell your possessions and give to the poor, and you will have treasure in heaven. Then come follow me." When the young man heard this, he went away sad, because he had great wealth.

The man who came to Jesus was a Jew, and he recognized our Savior as a teacher with authority. It is apparent that he had a grasp of the law, for he told Jesus that he was obedient to God's commands. We also know that he was wealthy, finding comfort and security in his possessions. This is revealed at the end of the conversation. From what we can determine, he was a good citizen and a religious man, who was concerned about spiritual matters. But there is a sense of works righteousness, meaning that he was trying to work his way into heaven through ritualistic obedience and good works. What is positive about the man's inquiry was his feeling that there was something lacking in his life.

This is a sad story, for it concerns an individual who was looking for salvation through the law. He was focused upon the outer life, rather than giving his heart to God through love and faith. It points out that people can be religious and still be far away from God. On the surface, many people appear to be Christians, but their heart has not changed. Outwardly they are religious, but inwardly there remains darkness. The Church is full of individuals who are simply going through the motions, believing that their life is spiritually intact. However, like the man in our story, some of these people may also feel that something is lacking.

An analysis of this man also reveals that he was a bargain hunter. Although he wanted to be saved, he was seeking a path that lacked real sacrifice. He said to Jesus, "What good thing must I do to get eternal life?" Note the singular tense of this question, as well as the implication of personal obligation. Even when Jesus told him to obey the commandments, he asked, "Which ones?" He was trying to do as little as possible to gain eternal life. After all, why obey all the commandments if it is not necessary. He wanted to know how much he could get away with and still receive the kingdom of God?

Jesus finally forced this wealthy man into a corner, from which there was no escape. He told Jesus that he obeyed all the commandments, and he wanted to know what else he must do. Jesus told him to sell all his possessions and give the money to the poor. Our Lord knew that the man's weakness related to his wealth, which became his spiritual demise. This, of course, presents some questions for us. What is our weakness? What are we willing to sacrifice for the kingdom of God? Are we really surrendering it all to Jesus Christ?

THE LAST DAYS

Matthew 24:36–44

> No one knows about that day or hour, not even the angels in heaven, nor the Son, but only the Father. As it was in the days of Noah, so it will be at the coming of the Son of Man. For in the days before the flood, people were eating and drinking, marrying and giving in marriage, up to the day Noah entered the ark; and they knew nothing about what would happen until the flood came and took them all away. That is how it will be at the coming of the Son of Man. Two men will be in the field; one will be taken and the other left. Therefore, keep watch, because you do not know on what day your Lord will come. But understand this; if the owner of the house had known at what time of the night the thief was coming, he would have kept watch and would not have let his house be broken into. So you also must be ready, because the Son of Man will come at an hour when you do not expect him.

As it was in the days of Noah, so shall it be when Jesus returns. It will be status quo, business as usual. In other words, there will be nothing to indicate that the end is near. Politicians will be giving their speeches, people will be investing in the stock market, and athletic events will be taking place. Jesus tells us that his return will be sudden and when least expected, and there will be no time to change our destiny. No one knows when this will occur, not the angels in heaven or the Son. This cosmic event is solely at the discretion of the Father. Try as we may to predict the Second Advent of Christ, it is simply impossible.

During the time of Noah evil was abounding, and God's warnings were unheeded. Like today, people refused to believe that they were accountable for their lives, and that one day there would be a judgment. The warnings given by the prophets, and later by the disciples, fell upon deaf ears. This response remains a reality today, for people continue to disregard God's warnings. The apostle Paul told believers that the time would come when people would cast aside sound doctrine and accept what suits their own desires, gathering around them teachers who will say what their itching ears want to hear. While this has always been true, many churches today have actually departed from orthodox beliefs. Those desiring to live in sin have compromised God's Word, while still claiming to be Christians.

Paul wrote that there would be terrible times in the last days. He said that people will be living wicked lifestyles, while appearing to be righteous. Also, in the last days there will be many false teachers, and people will fall away from the faith. As he did through the prophets during the time of Noah, the Lord continuously issues warnings through his servants and the written Word. Like loving parents warn their children against danger and destruction, God's warnings have been ceaseless.

The story of Noah reveals that everyone who entered the ark was saved from God's judgment upon the earth. In faith they obeyed the Lord, and their lives were spared. This same truth applies to everyone who enters God's kingdom through their faith in Jesus Christ. Like Noah and his family, they will escape the wrath that is to come. After Noah closed the door to the ark, the flood came, and the disobedient lost their lives. The ark would have saved them, but they lost their opportunity. When Jesus returns it will be a time of weeping and wailing for the unrepentant. So, why is it that people refuse to open their hearts to Christ? Why does the world cast aside the mercy of a loving God? Noah stepped out in faith, making preparation for God's judgment. What is our response to the Lord's warnings?

Nineteen

HOPE AND VICTORY

THE RACE FOR VICTORY

I Corinthians 9:24–27

> Do you not know that in a race all the runners run, but only one gets the prize? Run in such a way as to get the prize. Everyone who competes in the games goes into strict training. They do it to get a crown that will not last, but we do it to get a crown that will last forever. Therefore, I do not run like a man running aimlessly; I do not fight like a man beating the air. No, I beat my body and make it my slave, so that after I have preached to others, I myself will not be disqualified for the prize.

The city of Corinth was well-known for its athletic games, which evoked vivid images for Paul. They were images of exhaustive training, self-sacrifice, and endurance. In particular, Paul saw the runner as one who was finely tuned and willing to endure pain. These men gave their lives for the sport, knowing that victory only came to those who made the games their priority.

Paul was known for using human analogies to communicate spiritual truths, and this is one example of his creativity. Comparing Christianity to a race produces penetrating and descriptive insights into the challenges that we face as believers. Just as a race puts the total person to the test, we also are tested as we grow in Jesus Christ and walk in the Spirit. Everyday our faith, discipline, and commitment are put to the test by worldly influences and sin.

When reflecting upon this lesson, I was reminded of my high school days. I was never a good runner and dreaded going to the track to be timed for a grade. Being over six-foot tall and rather thin in those days, I had the potential to be a good runner, but that was not the case. I lacked the discipline and fortitude necessary for training and endurance. Also, I was not willing to endure the pain and expend the energy. This is the story of people when it comes to their spiritual life. They may start out with enthusiasm, but when the struggles come they begin to lose heart. This, of course, reveals a lack of faith in the strength that is promised by God. The prophet Isaiah wrote, "God gives strength to the weary, and increases the power of the weak. Those who hope in the Lord will renew their strength." The Lord offers us the sustaining grace that is needed to reach the finish line, but it takes faith and discipline to live in that grace.

Paul emphasizes that the crowns in this life will not last, but the crown God gives is eternal. What we do in the name of Jesus Christ will last forever; therefore, all effort must be given to stay in the race. The pain that we experience along the way cannot compare to the joy of crossing the finish line. For the Greeks, the race was the most thrilling event, even more exciting than the chariot races. It was the runner whose strength, stamina, and endurance were highly honored by the people. Homer wrote that "swiftness of foot is the most excellent endowment." Regardless of the pain, staying in the race and crossing the finish line was worth it. For us, finishing the race is not without its obstacles and struggles, but God's eternal kingdom is a prize that is worth any sacrifice. The Lord promises us the strength that we need to be victorious. The question is, are we willing to trust in God's promise of assured victory?

PROMISED BLESSINGS

Matthew 5:1–12

> Now when he saw the crowds, he went up on a mountainside and sat down. His disciples came to him, and he began to teach them, saying:
> "Blessed are the poor in spirit, for theirs is the kingdom of heaven.
> Blessed are those who mourn, for they will be comforted. Blessed are the meek, for they will inherit the earth. Blessed are those who hunger and thirst for righteousness, for they will be filled.
> Blessed are the merciful, for they will be shown mercy. Blessed are the pure in heart, for they will see God. Blessed are the peacemakers, for they will be called sons of God.
> Blessed are those who are persecuted because of righteousness, for theirs is the kingdom of heaven. Blessed are you when people insult you, persecute you and falsely say all kinds of evil against you because of me. Rejoice and be glad, for in the same way they persecuted the prophets who were before you."

The setting for this teaching is a beautiful hillside in Capernaum, which was a busy fishing village during the time of Jesus. It is also where our Savior spent considerable time teaching the people. On a trip to Israel, I stood on this hillside, recalling this wonderful message that Jesus shared with his disciples. Today, Capernaum is a place of tranquility where excavation is taking place. Two important excavations are the synagogue where Jesus taught in this small town, and the residence of the apostle Peter's mother-in-law.

The word *beatitude*, which Jesus uses in nine declarations, is rooted in Latin, and it means *supreme blessedness or happiness*. These are blessings from God that are bestowed upon those who share in the nature and mission of Jesus. Such blessings begin now and have their fulfillment in God's eternal kingdom.

Jesus began his homily of blessings and hope, by saying, "Blessed are the poor in spirit, for theirs is the kingdom of heaven." Who are the poor in spirit? At first glance, it seems that they are lacking some kind of life-giving force or will. However, in this context Jesus is referring to individuals who recognize their spiritual need. They know that apart from God's grace life is empty and powerless; therefore, they reach out to God in faith. Only the Lord can satisfy their innermost needs, and their life is one of total surrender. Jesus informed his disciples that the kingdom of God belongs to the poor in spirit.

Next, Jesus said, "Blessed are those who mourn, for they will be comforted." A person's mourning can result from many things that occur in life. We mourn over illness and the loss of loved ones. Many people mourn over the state of humanity and the world. They feel the weight of human suffering and the inhumanity that causes so many people to live in pain and deprivation. However, our Savior assures us that our burden for others will be lifted, for those who mourn will one day be comforted.

Jesus then said, "Blessed are the meek, for they will inherit the earth." The meek are individuals who humble themselves before the Lord and are gentle toward others. They show patience, tolerance, and understanding in the most difficult situations. Like Jesus, they are humble servants who are able to endure the insults of life. Jesus is their example, for even though he is the Son of God, he came to us as a humble servant who willingly sacrificed his life for our sins. Jesus calls us to walk in his footsteps for the sake of others and, if we are willing to follow, we will inherit the earth.

The fourth blessing speaks to those who hunger and thirst after righteousness, with the promise that they will be filled. To hunger after righteousness is to seek justice and equality for all people. It is to see others through the compassionate eyes of Christ. Regardless of what the injustice is, or where it occurs, the disciples of Jesus feel the pain of others, and they seek ways to relieve the suffering. It is through prayer, acts of love, and political action that righteousness is pursued. Our Savior informs us that one day there will be perfect justice.

Jesus continued his teaching with words for the merciful, promising that they will be shown mercy. We are not called by God because we are special people or learned theologians. Instead, we are called because of the heart of Jesus and his heart in us. Without grace no one would be saved. The prophet Isaiah wrote that our righteousness is like filthy rags, which simply means that our good works cannot save us. We are saved by God's mercy and our personal faith. But how can we expect the Lord's mercy, if we refuse to show mercy to others? Jesus tells us that it is the merciful that will be shown mercy from God.

The beatitudes continue with Jesus saying, "Blessed are the pure in heart, for they will see God." To be pure in heart is to seek only what is right in God's eyes. Our sole purpose is to please the Lord in all of our thoughts and actions. There are no self-serving motives, for we live for others and to the glory of God. Simply stated, to possess a pure heart is to have pure intentions and motives before God. Those who have a pure heart will one day see the Lord, for whom all glory is given.

In his blessings, Jesus also mentions the peacemakers, being those who make every effort to be at peace with all people. Peacemakers see no one as an enemy, for they know that every individual is precious in God's sight. They naturally communicate the peace of Christ, because his peace is in their hearts. God's peacemakers bring a sense of calm and healing in a world of anger and strife. Jesus tells us that these individuals are called the sons and daughters of God.

The last blessing focuses upon persecution that directly relates to being a witness for the gospel. The apostle Paul told his coworker Timothy that everyone who walks in the teachings of Christ will, in some way, experience persecution, and many people can attest to this truth. Some individuals find this within their family circles, while others may realize it through their profession. Persecution resulting from our Christian beliefs has many faces, but the ingredients are often emotional or verbal in nature. Sometimes people are ostracized from others or even physically attacked. The latter is more prevalent in certain parts of the world. But Jesus says that we should rejoice over such persecution, for we share in the heavenly rewards of the prophets who came before us.

When examining our Lord's homily, one realizes that the beatitudes comprise the virtues that speak to the Christian life. When considering them together, they manifest a life that has been transformed through the power of

Jesus Christ. Also, while the rewards may seem different, they all promise eternal life in God's kingdom. Jesus assures us that whatever suffering we endure in this life, it will be rewarded with eternal blessings. But have we truly received the Spirit of love and compassion? If so, are we allowing God's love to flow through us, that others might know his great mercy?

HOPE REALIZED

Psalm 62:5–8

> Find rest, O my soul, in God alone; my hope comes from him. He alone is my rock and my salvation; he is my fortress; I will not be shaken. My salvation and my honor depend on God; he is my mighty rock, my refuge. Trust in him at all times, O people; pour out your hearts to him, for God is our refuge.

Psalm sixty-two was written by King David and dedicated to the director of music for the temple. In this writing, David expresses absolute hope in the Lord. For David, God was both his rock and his place of refuge during times of trouble. Some authorities believe that this psalm was written during his son Absalon's rebellion, which was a tragedy for both David and the nation. Verse four of this psalm seems to allude to Absalon's intention to topple David from his throne. During Absalon's rebellion, both the kingdom and the nation were in turmoil, and David had to flee for his life. As evil took its toll, everything was falling apart. But David placed his hope in the Lord, knowing that God would provide the strength as well as the protection that he needed.

There are times in our lives when everything seems hopeless, and the world cannot help us. However, like David, we also have a tower of strength and a place of refuge. God is the same today as he was yesterday, and we can trust in his promises. David knew that he was clay in the Potter's hands, and that all hope was found in his Creator. The world will always let us down, but not the one who created the world. Just as God sustains his created order, he will also sustain us through those difficult times. When all appears hopeless, the Lord is there. Our frames are weak, but the Lord is a fortress where we can find safety from life's trials. David discovered that even your child can turn against you, especially when it involves wealth and power.

Paul told his fellow Christians that hope is connected to the inner life, and it is realized through a life that clings to Jesus Christ. Paul said, "If God is for us, who can be against us?" In other words, who or what can stand against one who walks with Christ? Those who cry out to the Lord in humility and faith will be heard, which is a lesson that Job learned from God's own mouth. Whether in life or death, the Lord is with the faithful. Jesus tells us that he will never abandon us, and we can trust this promise.

But how can we develop hope if we refuse to allow God's full reign over our lives? In the desert the Israelites had to completely trust God, which was not easy for them to do. They repeatedly lost hope, experiencing the devastating results. Sometimes this is the situation with us. When we try to live without God, we learn that nothing satisfies our deepest needs. It is the believing and patient heart that is assured of God's presence. The Lord's grace takes us through life one step at a time, providing certain hope along the way.

TRIUMPH OVER TEMPTATION

Luke 4:1–13

> Jesus, full of the Holy Spirit, returned from the Jordan and was led by the Spirit in the desert, where for forty days he was tempted by the devil. He ate nothing during those days, and at the end of them he was hungry. The devil said to him, "If you are the Son of God, tell this stone to become bread." Jesus answered, "It is written: 'Man does not live on bread alone.'" The devil led him up to a high place and showed him in an instant all the kingdoms of the world. And he said to him, "I will give you all their authority and splendor, for it has been given to me, and I can give it to anyone I want to. So if you worship me, it will all be yours." Jesus answered, "It is written: 'Worship the Lord your God, and serve him only.'" The devil led him to Jerusalem and had him stand on the highest point of the temple. "If you are the Son of God," he said, "throw yourself down from here. For it is written: 'He will command his angels concerning you, to guard you carefully; they will lift you up in their hands, so that you will not strike your foot against a stone.'" Jesus answered, "It says: 'Do not put the Lord your God to the test.'" When the devil had finished all this tempting, he left him until an opportune time.

Luke tells us that Jesus was filled with the Holy Spirit, yet Satan relentlessly tempted him during his forty days in the wilderness. This reveals that the most Spirit-filled people will never be free from temptation. Regardless of where we are on our spiritual journey, we are not exempt from Satan's attacks. Actually, the closer we are to the Lord, the more severe the attacks may be. The destruction of godly people is unquestionably a victory for the devil. But some people do not believe this reality, claiming that Christians are on protected ground. The truth, of course, is the opposite, for followers of Christ are tempted everyday. Many temptations are not as obvious as others, such as the temptation not to love and forgive people. There are also those temptations relating to pride, power, and self-righteousness. A temptation that we seldom think about is that of spiritual complacency.

In the desert Jesus experienced physical temptations, as well as Satan's attempts to implant the desire for self-elevation and worldly power. If you noted, the devil even tried to get Jesus to put God, the Father, to the test. But in his attempt to thwart God's will and plan of salvation for the world, Satan primarily tempted Jesus to think only about his own needs. His method was to create doubt and arouse pride and self-will. After all, we must take care of ourselves!

The temptations that faced Jesus are the same attacks that we face. Although they are often subtle, their power must be recognized and confronted. It is important that each person search their hearts to examine the desires and motives that are destructive. We must stand strong in our fight against the devil, realizing both the personal and collective results of our responses.

Faith in God's Word and promise is our primary weapon against Satan's attacks. In his response to the devil, Jesus repeatedly answered by quoting the Scriptures. He fought off Satan with his faith and the truth found in the Word. When we are tempted, do we exercise our faith in God and the power of his Word?

PALMS OF VICTORY

John 12:12–15

> The next day the great crowd that had come from the Feast heard that Jesus was on his way to Jerusalem. They took palm branches and went out to meet him, shouting, "Hosanna!" "Blessed is he who comes in the name of the Lord! Blessed is the King of Israel." Jesus found a young donkey and sat upon it, as it is written, "Do not be afraid, O Daughter of Zion; see your king is coming, seated on a donkey's colt."

The Jewish leaders were justified in believing that the miracles Jesus performed would cause problems. People were coming from all over the region to get a glimpse of the man that many thought was God's Messiah. Like a popular politician, the people were curiously drawn to Jesus. After all, this was the Passover season that celebrated Israel's exodus out of Egyptian slavery. It was believed that God would send the Messiah during a Passover celebration, and Jesus might be the one. Who else could speak with God's authority and perform such miracles, including raising the dead?

Jesus' entry into Jerusalem was understood as a victory march for a national hero. He was even hailed by some as their king, who would somehow free them from Roman occupation and bondage. The apostle John tells us that the people chanted, *Hosanna,* which is translated *save now.* If only they had known that Jesus would soon be arrested and crucified.

John states that the people were waving palm branches, which was significant in this situation. Palm trees were important to the Middle East, primarily because of the many products that came from them. These trees can reach a height of one hundred feet, and they had numerous uses during the time of Christ. Because of their significance, the palm trees became symbolic of everything that is good. Sketches of palm trees were found in the decor of the tabernacle and temple, and ancient coins and tombs had engravings of palm trees. At certain times in Israel's history, the waving of palm branches became a cultural expression of victory, joy, and peace. The Jewish historian Josephus wrote that heroes and dignitaries were greeted into Jerusalem with the waving of palms.

As Jesus rode into Jerusalem on a foal, the people lined the road waving palm branches. They were expressing joy and anticipation, believing that Jesus was a deliverer sent by God. Their focus, however, was upon a worldly and political deliverer. Apparently few people understood that Jesus came to offer salvation through repentance and faith in him. They were blinded by sin, being unable to look within themselves and beyond the earthly realm. The Jewish people wanted a deliverer, but their minds and hearts were on the temporal and temporary. This could have been a special Passover, had the people only recognized Jesus as the Son of God. But things have not changed, for people are still focusing upon the world, rather than their inner life and eternal destiny. They are capable of seeing truth, but their hearts are in the wrong place. The world is still searching for another way to salvation. How many people in the present can wave palms, declaring their victory in Jesus Christ?

SORROW FOR THE DEAD

I Thessalonians 4:13–18

> Brothers, we do not want you to be ignorant about those who fall asleep, or to grieve like the rest of men, who have no hope. We believe that Jesus died and rose again, and so we believe that God will bring with Jesus those who have fallen asleep in him. According to the Lord's own word, we tell you that we who are still alive, who are left till the coming of the Lord, will certainly

not precede those who have fallen asleep. For the Lord himself will come down from heaven, with a loud command, with the voice of the archangel and with the trumpet call of God, and the dead in Christ will rise first. After that, we who are still alive and are left will be caught up with them in the clouds to meet the Lord in the air. And so we will be with the Lord forever. Therefore encourage each other with these words.

Job asked the question, "When a person dies, will they live again?" There is something in us that hungers for eternal life. Somehow we refuse to believe that our death ends everything. If our funeral is the conclusion of life, then what was the purpose of our birth and life on earth? Over the years we have heard and read many things about death experiences that have strengthened our Christian beliefs. Medical professionals and patients have reported situations when clinical death revealed the continuation of life. After having died, people report hovering over their bodies in operating rooms, providing detailed descriptions that could only be seen from above. Some people say that they saw deceased relatives, or even conversed with Jesus while they were in this state.

The Thessalonians knew that the dead in Christ would rise again, but they were saddened to think that departed saints would not take part in the glorious return of Jesus Christ. But Paul informed them that those who died in Christ will participate in this apocalyptic event. In fact, he assured them that the dead in Christ will rise first and be gathered around Jesus at his appearance. Paul added that those who are alive when Jesus returns will be transformed and caught up in the air to meet Christ and the gathered saints.

It is interesting that Paul speaks about the departed as having fallen asleep. The Greek translation indicates both a present and future awakening, which affirms that there is never a cessation of life. Whether we are literally asleep prior to our Lord's return, or in a blissful state of consciousness, we are alive in Jesus Christ. Sleep does not mean the end of life, but simply unconsciousness to earthly surroundings. Like Lazarus, those who fall asleep are in God's realm, where they only hear his voice. When Lazarus died he was unconscious to earthly surroundings, but he heard Jesus calling him out of the tomb.

There is always sorrow over the loss of a loved one, for love and sorrow are intertwined. But in the midst of our sorrow and pain there is certain hope. It is a hope that is based upon the resurrection of Jesus Christ, and his promise that we also will rise to eternal life. Our death removes the veil and brings us into God's glory. It is the triumphant entry into the everlasting kingdom, where tears and sadness are replaced with victory and joy. Paul wanted believers to know that those who fall asleep in Christ are secure, and they will not miss the glory of our Lord's return. This is a message of encouragement and hope for everyone, both the living and the departed.

HE HAS RISEN

Mark 16:1–8

> When the Sabbath was over, Mary Magdalene, Mary the mother of James, and Salome, brought spices so that they might go to anoint Jesus' body. Very early on the first day of the week, just after sunrise, they were on their way to the tomb, and they asked each other, "Who will roll away the stone from the entrance of the tomb?" But when they looked up, they saw that the stone, which was very large, had been rolled away. As they entered the tomb, they saw a young man dressed in a white robe sitting on the right side, and they were alarmed. "Don't be alarmed," he said "You are looking for Jesus the Nazarene, who was crucified. He has risen! He is not here. See the place where they laid him. But go, tell his disciples and Peter, 'He is going ahead of you into Galilee. There you will see him, just as he told you.'" Trembling and bewildered, the women went out and fled from the tomb. They said nothing to anyone, because they were afraid.

At dawn, three women went to our Lord's tomb to anoint his body with spices. It was a mission of love and deep respect for the one who had changed their life. But instead of a decaying body, the women found an empty tomb. The huge stone had been rolled back, and the soldiers that had been guarding the tomb had fled in fear. Then came the announcement from a man dressed in white, who was sitting on the right side of the tomb. He told the women that Jesus Christ had risen from the dead, just as he said he would. This announcement to the women was the first Easter message given to the world.

The women came to anoint Jesus' body, for in death they still loved him and wanted to say their final farewell. But instead of finding death, they were given a message of life. In this tomb of sorrow, they received the hope of resurrection glory. The angel told them that Jesus was not there, but he assured them that they would see him again. What a message of hope! Jesus told his disciples that he would rise from the dead, but this claim was certainly met with confusion. Now, however, as impossible as it seemed, Jesus' words were understood.

The proof of the resurrection is not simply found in the empty tomb and the angel's announcement, but also in the many eyewitness accounts of the apostles and other believers. Jesus' appearances continued for forty days before his visible ascension into heaven. What followed was the preaching of the gospel throughout the region. According to tradition, all the apostles, except John, were martyred for their faith. This fact alone assures us that they had seen the risen Christ, for it is incomprehensible that they would have died for a lie.

The most powerful witness today for our Savior's resurrection is the Holy Spirit, who was promised by Jesus. The presence of the Spirit in our hearts and lives bears witness to the risen Lord, telling us that Jesus has conquered sin and death. It is the Holy Spirit who brings us the gifts of understanding, faith, and power. Through the Spirit's leading we walk the path of Jesus, surrendering our lives for God's message of hope, while awaiting our Savior's glorious return. The question is, are we being obedient to God's call? Do we have the certain hope that is found in Jesus Christ?

IN A LITTLE WHILE

John 16:16–23

> Jesus said, "In a little while you will see me no more, and then after a little while you will see me." Some of his disciples said to one another, "What does he mean by saying, 'In a little while you will see me no more, and then after a little while you will see me,' and 'Because I am going to the Father'?" They kept asking, "What does he mean by 'a little while'? We don't understand what he is saying." Jesus saw that they wanted to ask him about this, so he said to them, "Are you asking one another what I mean when I said, 'In a little while you will see me no more, and then after a little while you will see me'? I tell you the truth, you will weep and mourn while the world rejoices. You will grieve, but your grief will turn to joy. A woman giving birth to a child has pain because her time has come; but when her baby is born she forgets the anguish because of her joy that a child is born into the world. So with you: Now is your time of grief, but I will see you again and you will rejoice, and no one will take away your joy. In that day you will no longer ask me anything. I tell you the truth, my Father will give you whatever you ask in my name."

In these verses Jesus repeatedly speaks about his departure and subsequent return, and the apostles wanted an explanation. They did not realize that he was preparing them for his death and resurrection. When Jesus died on the cross he was physically taken from them, and the interval between his death and resurrection was a time of grief and pain. For others, however, it was a time of rejoicing. The religious leaders and Roman officials saw Jesus as someone who challenged their authority. To be rid of him would once again bring peace and order to the area.

But what the authorities were expecting did not last long, for Jesus rose from the dead just as he promised. Not only was there an empty tomb, but the disciples and others would soon see Jesus in the flesh. What began with the consuming grief of the crucifixion, the bitter end of their Master, would soon be overshadowed by the glory of his resurrection. In the midst of their pain, God's truth and love was revealed. What seemed to be the end of hope was only the beginning. In Jesus Christ life overcame death, and eternity in God's kingdom became a clear message for believers.

The disciples worshipped Jesus when they saw him, and they were filled with joy. His resurrection removed their doubt and fear, empowering them to proclaim the gospel of the risen Christ. When Jesus rose from the dead, the disciples knew that he had the power to fulfill all his promises. Over time they became aware of the prophecies in the Hebrew Scriptures that pointed to Christ. All the pieces of the puzzle began to fit into place. The path was now before them, for they were commissioned by Jesus to take his truth into the world.

Jesus has returned to the Father, but in a little while we will see him. Our Savior has promised that he will return for the saints. Whether it is those who have already died in Christ, or people living at the time of his return, everyone will see the risen Lord. Jesus said, "I am coming quickly, and my reward is with me, to render to every person according to what they have done." One day the sky will be rolled back, and every eye will see Jesus in the clouds of heaven. The Church is now going through its *little while* of sorrow and suffering, but we are assured of our Savior's return. We must never lose hope, for in *a little while* Jesus will appear, bringing all sorrow to an end.

THE HEAVENS WILL SHAKE

Mark 13:24–27

> But in those days, following that distress, the sun will be darkened, and the moon will not give its light; the stars will fall from the sky, and the heavenly bodies will be shaken. At that time men will see the Son of Man coming in the clouds with great power and glory. And he will send his angels and gather his elect from the four winds, from the ends of the earth to the ends of the heavens. Now learn this lesson from the fig tree: As soon as its leaves come out, you know that summer is near. Even so, when you see these things happening,

you know that it is near, right at the door. I tell you the truth, this generation will not pass away until these things have happened. Heaven and earth will pass away, but my words will never pass away.

When Jesus returns the sun will be darkened, the moon will lose its light, the stars will fall from the sky, and the heavenly bodies will be shaken. When these cosmic events take place, Jesus will appear in the clouds of heaven, in a manner that all eyes will see him. Every person from every age will witness the glory of the Lord's return. The Second Advent of Christ will bring this age to an end. There will be a new heaven and a new earth, and the righteous will enter into God's eternal kingdom. The dead in Christ will rise first, and those who are alive will be raptured to meet Jesus and the saints in the air. No longer will there be sadness and tears, and death will be swallowed up in victory.

Like a loving parent warns a child, the Lord is telling us to be prepared. From the time of the apostles until the present, humanity has had knowledge of Jesus' return, when he will judge the world and give the saints their eternal reward. But people either reject this truth, or believe that they have time to repent and turn their lives around. Even if the Scriptures are true, they think that there will be time to acknowledge Christ and be saved. Jesus, however, states that there is no time, for his return will be sudden and when least expected. It will occur as quick as a flash of lightning, and no one will have time to change their destiny. Jesus emphasizes that his return will be like a thief in the night, with no one knowing the day or hour. Besides, to think that you can accept Jesus at the last minute is simply an attempt to manipulate and deceive the Lord.

The world belongs to God, and we are his stewards and servants, who will one day be called to accountability. God's grace has provided us with gifts and opportunities that bring responsibilities. It is out of love that we have been warned, for the Lord seeks to save everyone from sin and eternal death. But rather than understanding Jesus' message as one of love, some people receive it as a threat and ultimatum. This tragic response, which is the result of pride, blocks the grace that God is offering. Just as we don't know when Jesus will return, we also lack knowledge concerning our health and time of death. The opportunity to receive Jesus Christ and serve God is not guaranteed beyond this moment. This is why the author of Hebrews wrote, "Today, if you hear his voice, do not harden your hearts." We must always examine our hearts, knowing the uncertainty of life and that the return of Christ is imminent. Jesus said, "What I say to you, I say to everyone—Watch!"

ETERNAL GLORY

Isaiah 35:4–10

> Be strong, do not fear; your God will come, he will come with vengeance; with divine retribution he will come to save you. Then the eyes of the blind will be opened, and the ears of the deaf unstopped. Then will the lame leap like a deer, and the tongue of the dumb shout for joy. Water will gush forth in the wilderness and streams in the desert. The burning sand will become a pool, the thirsty ground bubbling springs. In the haunts where jackals once lay, grass and reeds and papyrus will grow. And a highway will be there; it will be called the Way of Holiness. The unclean will not journey on it; it will be for those who walk in that Way; wicked fools will not go about on it. No lion will be there, nor will any ferocious beast get up on it; they will not be found there. But only the redeemed will walk there, and the ransomed of the Lord will return. They will enter Zion with singing, everlasting joy will crown their heads. Gladness and joy will overtake them, and sorrow and sighing will flee away.

What you just read is God's eternal promise for those who walk in righteousness. Although this passage was partially fulfilled in Israel's deliverance from Babylon, it points forward to the peace and joy of God's everlasting kingdom. The prophetic words of Isaiah clearly speak about a time beyond this present age. This is the language of complete deliverance from a world in which disobedience and sin has robbed the people of peace and joy. Isaiah wrote, "They will enter Zion with singing, everlasting joy will crown their heads. Gladness and joy will overtake them, and sorrow and sighing will flee away." Isaiah encouraged the people to be strong, for the Lord will come. This is the Second Advent of Christ, which will usher in God's glorious promise for all who have kept the faith through life's trials and tribulations.

Throughout their history, the Israelites continually experienced the presence of God. They were aware of his love, as well as the wrath that resulted from their disobedience. This passage of scripture addresses both the judgment and the mercy of God. Verse eight is quite insightful, for it speaks about a highway named the Way. This verse specifically relates to Jesus, who is the way to the Father. In fact, it was for this reason that the early Church was called the *Way*. Jesus is the highway that takes us to God's everlasting kingdom, which the Jews symbolically referred to as Zion. Isaiah was telling the people that the embodiment of the Lord would come to earth and be our path to heaven. This prophecy began with the birth of Christ and will be fulfilled at his Second Advent. It is *Emmanuel,* meaning "God with us," who is showing us the way to the Father.

Isaiah's words were given to take away our anxieties and fears, by emphasizing God's promise of eternal life in his kingdom. It is a prophecy of deliverance from a world torn apart from the destructiveness of sin. Isaiah is reminding us that the one who created us out of love will deliver us. This is a promise that begins now for those who have received Jesus as their Lord and Savior. Jesus told his disciples that they were not to fear, for he would always be with them, bringing light into a world of darkness.

Like most children, I experienced anxiety when the lights were turned out in my bedroom. It made me feel alone and helpless. I no longer fear physical darkness, but I do fear the thought of spiritual darkness and the thought of not being able to enter the holy city of Zion. The apostle John wrote, "Blessed are those who have washed their robes, and may go through the gates into the eternal city."

CONCLUSION

This book has been a labor of love and my spiritual food for almost two years. While writing each section, the Holy Spirit stirred my heart, bringing me into a reflective mode. I examined my life in the light of each passage of scripture and the lessons that they hold for daily living. I particularly thought about my relationships, and how the Lord was moving me to love others more. I also came to realize the need for increased study and understanding, as well as the importance to prayerfully meditate upon biblical teachings, especially those of our Savior. I encourage each of you to embrace this same reflective process, promising that you will be blessed as you experience the heart and mind of Jesus.

The Scriptures are not simply a guide to help us through life, but rather the spiritual diet that we need to walk with the Lord. When reading God's Word, I am always amazed how new channels open for increased understanding and personal development. The Bible takes us from shallow waters to a depth that no theologian will ever reach. This is both the mystery and the glory of God's written Word. While all scripture is divinely inspired with the intent of changing our lives, it is the teachings of Jesus Christ and the apostles that bring us into the Lord's saving grace, setting before us the path of life. Their words satisfy our deepest needs, providing the certain hope that keeps us firm in our faith and commitment.

This book was written to encourage and challenge us to spiritually grow and become one with our Savior. To read these teachings without internalizing their life-changing truths is to lose the grace intended by God.

About the Author

HENRY G. COVERT is an ordained minister with the United Church of Christ. He is the author of *Ministry to the Incarcerated* and has served as an adjunct professor at The Pennsylvania State University. His recent book *Discovering the Parables* was published by Praeger in 2007.

MORE BY DR. HENRY G. COVERT

Discovering the Parables
Long before there were printing presses, copy machines, and email, societies used storytelling to convey beliefs, history, and traditions. This practice preceded the ministry of Jesus and continues today in many cultures. Jesus was a master storyteller. His words provide guidelines and a road map for living, as well as the insights for spiritual understanding and personal development. Using familiar imagery found in nature and other recognizable sources, He engaged His listeners with lessons that confronted every aspect of their lives, providing the tools for self-examination and change. This book speaks to the heart! *(144pp. Masthof Press, 2023.) $12.00*

Exploring Christianity
In a succinct and direct manner, the author takes the reader on a journey from the creation story to the end of this age. He offers insights into essential Christian doctrines, providing some of the differences between faith groups. In clear detail he explains the meaning of Jesus' crucifixion, as well as the many proofs of His resurrection. The contemporary Church is also examined, revealing its challenges and the changes that are necessary. This book is enlightening, speaking to our understanding and spiritual development. It is an excellent resource for individuals and the Church. *(181pp. Masthof Press, 2023.) $12.00*

Journey To The Next World: Understanding Death & Resurrection
Death and the afterlife speak to everyone. Dr. Covert examines our life journey from different perspectives, including the biblical understanding of death and resurrection and the events leading to the Second Advent of Jesus. He reminds us of the many obstacles and destructive forces that are encountered as we journey to our heavenly home. The reader is urged to make preparation by nourishing the inner life with the gifts of the Holy Spirit. This book is educational, spiritually motivating, and encouraging. *(139pp. Masthof Press, 2022.) $12.00*

More on next page!

Ministry to the Incarcerated

Dr. Covert uses his experiences as both police officer and state prison chaplain to examine the environment of the incarcerated—people who are often forgotten by society. He emphasizes particular areas of inmate stress and how they impact upon the inmate's spiritual formation and the role of the Church in offering encouragement, healing and transformation. He calls for staff education, environmental improvement, and a pastoral presence that facilitates rehabilitation and hope, rather than discouragement and punishment. *(185pp. index. Masthof Press, 2022) $12.00*

Prayers That God Hears

The misconceptions relating to prayer make it a topic that is often abstract and difficult to understand. Dr. Covert's treatment of the subject is both biblically rooted and realistic. The simplicity of this book brings a clarity and continuity that is easily grasped and applied to one's life. It answers our questions and speaks to our deepest needs and struggles. This book is for everyone who seeks a meaningful relationship with God and others. *(140pp. Masthof Press, 2022) $12.00*

Spiritual Insights

Dr. Covert explores the important themes of the Bible, placing them in a topical format that is easy to read and understand. Each topic is expanded in ways that speak to the reader's spiritual questions and development. This is an excellent book for personal devotion, as well as a valuable tool for preaching and teaching. *(123pp. Masthof Press, 2023.) $12.00*

www.ingramcontent.com/pod-product-compliance
Lightning Source LLC
Chambersburg PA
CBHW070057080526
44586CB00013B/1103